Around The World In 37 Days:

What I Learned From The Poorest And The Richest

Around The World In 37 Days:

What I Learned From The Poorest And The Richest

By Leroy Martin

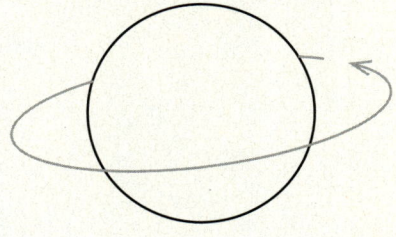

*This book is dedicated to all the friendly folks whom
I had the opportunity of meeting and who treated
me as one of their lifelong friends throughout
my short journey across the globe.*

The world is a book, and those who do not travel read only one page

— Saint Augustine

Table of Contents

Around The World In 37 Days:

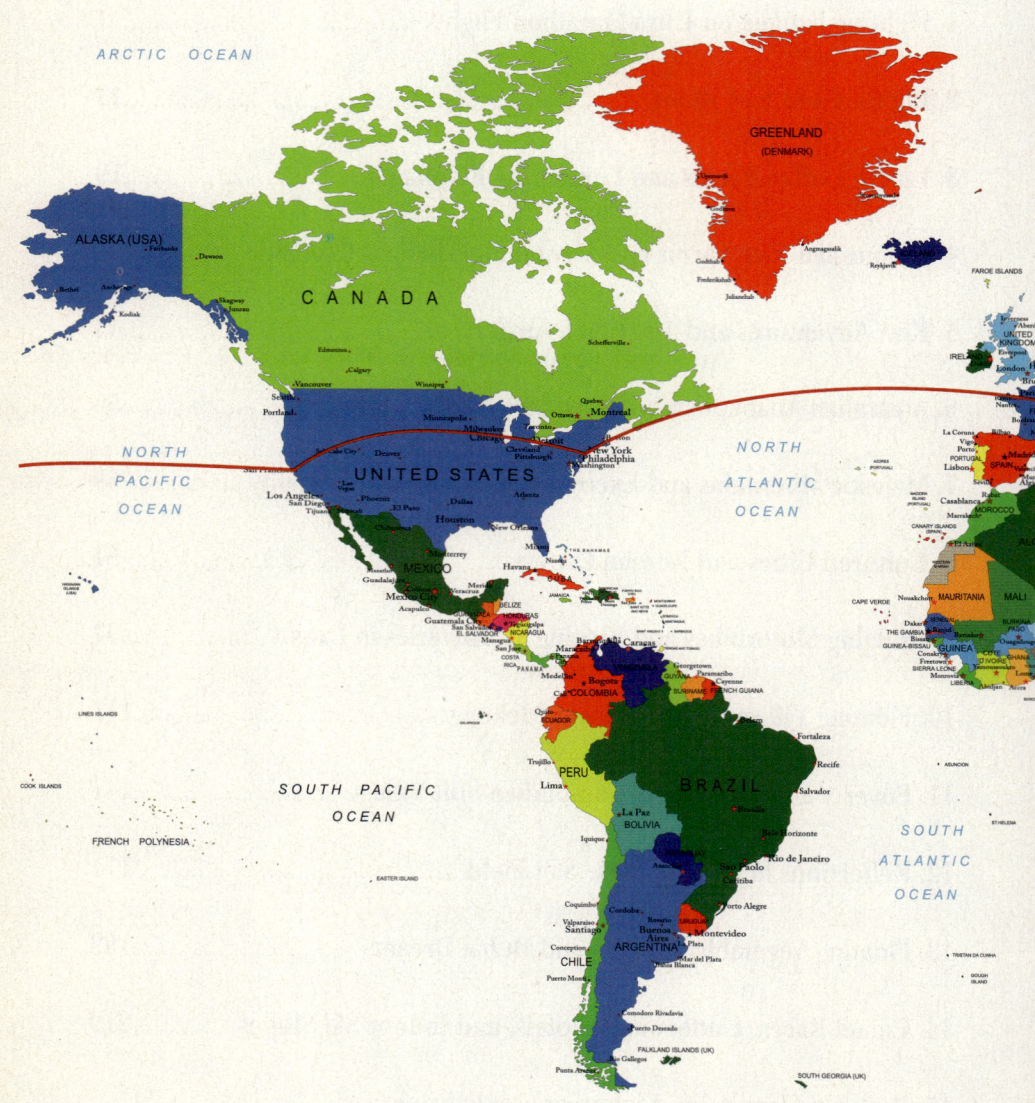

The author began his journey in New Jersey's Newark Liberty International Airport, and then flew to San Francisco International Airport. From there the journey resumed across the Pacific Ocean to Singapore. He then visited the following countries in chronological order: Thailand, Malaysia, Indonesia, Australia, New Zealand, Tasmania (Australian

What I Learned From
The Poorest And The Richest

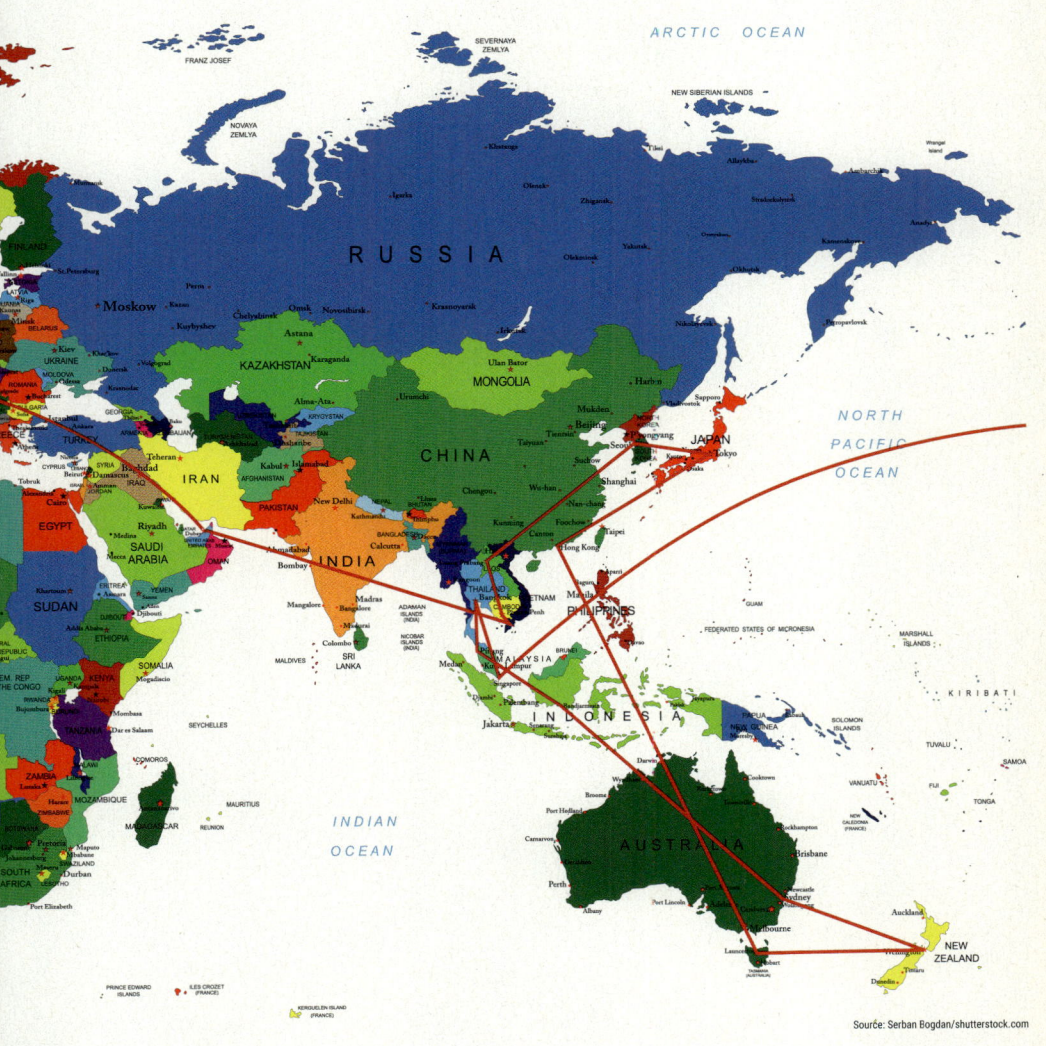

Source: Serban Bogdan/shutterstock.com

Island), Hong Kong, Japan, South Korea, Laos, Cambodia, Vietnam, and the United Arab
Emirates (Dubai). From Dubai, the author jetted eastward across portions of Europe prior
to touching down on the New Jersey tarmac.

ACKNOWLEDGMENTS

It takes a village to publish a book. Prior to this project, I hadn't always seen it that way. I admired authors, believing that they were immeasurably motivated and had somehow tapped into a boundless well of inspiration. While this may be true for some, the same isn't necessarily true for me. In fact, if it hadn't been for the relentless encouragement of a few of my close friends and colleagues, you would very likely not be holding this book in your hands.

Throughout this project, I required a significant amount of encouragement to continue. For those who know me well, it is no secret that I can occasionally—too often—become distracted by projects and failing to see them arrive at a fruitful conclusion is not necessarily uncommon. Bearing this in mind, it is only appropriate that I would acknowledge the names of the people who have been involved with this project or who have been a wonderful influence on me throughout the years.

This isn't actually my book. Yes, I have written it and labored intensely for countless hours, utilizing mental energy and creativity which were integrated onto the following pages, but any recognition for this book belongs as much to the following people as it does to me.

The highest acknowledgments must be reserved for God, the Giver of all talents and Creator of all living things, whom I depend on for fresh mercies every morning. My nephew Jeffrey (my traveling partner) and I are grateful that we were granted a safe journey.

To my dear parents, thank you for everything you have done for me throughout my life. While I was a scholar and desired to devour books voraciously rather than pull my share of the workload on the home farm, you exercised patience more times than could possibly be counted. Despite my congenital affinity towards books, you wisely reminded me that a boy must also perform physical labor, and you somehow managed to instill a respectable work ethic in me. I am especially grateful to both of you for having passed along a genuine interest in people groups who are vastly different than our own. I strongly believe that your inherent interest in people groups throughout the world has infused me.

To my employer, Raymond Lapp. Thank you for your invaluable advice regarding not only within the publishing industry, but also as a mentor of sorts. As of 2019, I have enjoyed several years of employment at Plain Communities Business Exchange (a monthly business publication primarily for folks within the diverse Plain communities throughout North America and beyond). It is enjoyable being a part of the growing team of individuals who seek to serve the various needs of business owners within these communities. I consider it a privilege to have become acquainted with you and your wonderful family.

To Andrew, my colleague and graphics designer. I am indebted to the excellent service which you provided for the duration of this project. Without your assistance, this book would fail to captivate or appeal to anyone. Thank you for the countless hours for which you painstakingly labored, so that I could have a book to share with a few people regarding my memorable travel experiences while traversing around the globe.

To Jimmy, a distant friend and former colleague. Without your constant reminders for me to continue with this project, I doubt that I would have been as diligent. You held me accountable to my projected timetables with fierce resolve, for which I am grateful. There was no slacking with you peering over my shoulder—from afar. Your admonishments were needed, and I thank you.

Whenever I doubted myself and my work, you believed in me, which I appreciated greatly, but considered to be quite risky of you.

To John, a colleague and friend. The wheels of my return flight from this journey had not even touched the ground before you began discussing book deals with me. I remember all too well your suggestion of authoring a book while talking with you on the phone during my visit to Cambodia. As I stood outside my hotel early one morning watching several stray chickens and roosters pierce the parched Cambodian soil for a bite to eat during our phone call, you reminded me that you considered it imperative that I would at least consider documenting my experiences for a future book project. Thanks for your encouragement and continued assistance with this project.

To Ivan Lee, a colleague. Thank you for assisting with the proofreading, your sharp eye helped to identify a few problem areas.

To Lavern, a neighbor and friend. Yours was the last familiar face we saw for more than five weeks. You accompanied Jeffery and I to the airport the day of our departure. I remember thinking that perhaps I am attempting too dangerous of a journey when we said our goodbyes moments before boarding a flight headed to the other side of the world. You assured Jeffrey and I that everything should work out fine, but I still had my doubts. Turns out you were right, we had a wonderful and safe journey, for which we are grateful for. Thank you for your prayers.

To Wilson, a neighbor and friend. You were so eager to see me return home after my thirty-seven-day excursion, that you jumped on a passenger train and met Jeffrey and I at the Newark Liberty International Airport in New Jersey. Your smiling face was the first familiar countenance which we saw upon arriving to our homeland. We had been exhausted from our travels, still wrestling with formidable jet lag, courtesy of a significant time zone deficit, however, all that seemed to disappear as we gathered around a table in the middle of the bustling airport to catch up on each other's adventures which had transpired since we had last seen each other. Thank you for urging me to write this book.

To Leon at SRS. Thank you for providing a cozy office space so that I could work on this project, sometimes late into the night.

To my nephew Jeffrey. Thank you for being the best travel partner I could have hoped for. You were excited to travel with me to vastly unfamiliar lands while learning about different cultures and practices. This excitement was not, however, met without a healthy dose of apprehension. I will never forget how uncomfortable you were while walking through the slums of Malaysia. Upon reflection, I should have been more mindful of your valid concerns instead of throwing caution to the wind and foolishly relishing in the potential dangers which the moment presented. Thanks also for being patient with me throughout the journey.

To my friend Nevin. Thanks for everything you have done for me throughout the years. Several years ago, you began encouraging me to write. Initially, I wasn't sure that I would like to dedicate the amount of time required to write extensively, however, I have grown fond of attempting to stitch words together. Thank you for your friendship and the valuable life lessons which you have taught me.

To Jason, a neighbor and friend. You and I discussed this project for countless hours. I agonized over many details, yet you reminded me everything will be ok. Thanks for listening and providing practical input.

To my fifth-grade teacher Edna. Thanks for having been a great geography teacher as well as permitting me to indulge in the school library's collection. I read books about the Asian and African continents with great zeal whenever I was caught up with my class assignments. It is there, in that one-room schoolhouse many years ago, that I became insatiably fascinated with cultures and practices of other humans whom I share this planet with.

In conclusion, a special thank you to all the friends, family, colleagues, etc., who had been praying for our safety throughout our journey. To anyone else whom I may regrettably have forgotten to mention formally, rest assured any oversight on my part wasn't intentional.

FOREWORD

A few messages from the author's family, friends, and colleagues

While living in rural southern Ohio and having my days filled with carpentry and farming, my adventurous spirit began to get restless. Having heard some of my uncle Leroy's fascinating stories of the journeys he has taken across the globe, made it all the more enticing.

Upon his return from visiting twenty-six countries in Europe during December/January 2018, I requested that Leroy would consider taking me along on his next overseas adventure. He did not resist my suggestion. Needless to say, after months of planning and dreaming, this amazing trip around the world began to take shape. As our departure date drew closer, I became increasingly apprehensive. All the *what ifs* began to fill my mind, but I knew my sidekick had done this time and time again. So, I told myself to quit all the stressing.

Experiencing my first plane ride was a trip in and of itself. Seeing the Colorado Rockies from the air and flying above the clouds made me feel like a small person indeed. After our flight from California to Singapore, with a thirteen-hour time difference, made us look and feel like we were dazed people.

Getting introduced to a whole new line of food was one of the first things we experienced. While walking through a market, it was a common sight to see all kinds of food hanging in the hot sun, with countless amounts of flies swarming around. While some things took my appetite, we did learn to enjoy the native foods. The pastries in Japan were finger-licking good.

New Zealand seemed more like home to me, with their farming industry and abundant numbers of cattle. Seeing how the Indonesian's make ends meet by mostly raising produce and rice was an eye-opener. Some of our taxi rides have no words to describe them! Drivers who were unaccustomed to our language and definitely do not have the same traffic laws that we have in the States, caused us to sit on the edge of our seat. While on the other hand, we also met some drivers who went the extra mile for us and were exceptionally helpful.

One of my favorite places which we visited was Cambodia. Where they have stilt villages, due to their rainy seasons. During our trip, we had the opportunity to see their school in action. So neat, but of course, very different. It was rewarding to see their excited faces as we gave them the coloring books we had purchased.

Their floating village will be forever etched in my memory! Having a school, police station, church, and various grocery stores floating on a body of water.

It was not uncommon to have little children approach us, begging for money. Seeing that outstretched hand, hearing "dollar, dollar;" made it difficult to resist giving them money. However, in majority of places, we were sternly told not to give money to the children because it only encourages the begging.

We experienced culture shocks from being in Third World countries, and then flying into extremely wealthy Dubai, which is located within the middle of a desert. Fancy skyscrapers, underwater hotels, and indoor ski slopes made me think of those happy, poor people in Southeast Asia. They hardly had anything, yet were still the friendliest, happy, and hospitable folks.

Being in thirteen different countries and seeing many walks of life made it clear that we Americans have much to be thankful for.

A special thank you to Uncle Leroy for giving me this opportunity to join him on this adventure and to make my traveling dreams come true. It was truly time well spent and an unforgettable trip.

And now to my family and friends; thank you for the many prayers which you said regarding our safety.

To everyone else; I sincerely hope that you enjoy reading about the different cultures and interesting people groups whom we met along our whirlwind journey around the world.

~*Jeffrey Martin*

Having never traveled abroad, I found this book very interesting. Especially since reading of the countries which we had learned about while studying geography in school many years ago. The information on the terraces planted with rice was very fascinating, as was the visit with the Anabaptist community in Tasmania. Even though riding the bullet trains in Japan would be exciting, the rest of Japan must be beautiful for the scenery.

As a scholar, Leroy would write many stories, so it comes naturally for him to be having this talent of writing.

This was an excellent way to hear and see of far-off lands. Reading of God's differently created countries was interesting. It behooves us to be thankful for all we have. Let us always be grateful for our freedom of worship, speech, and everything our Lord sees fit.

~*Florence Martin (the author's mother)*

This book is written by a friend Leroy Martin while living on a small farm in rural Pennsylvania. He enjoys feeding the farm animals and helping the farm boss harvest the bountiful crops raised on the farm! He enjoys the seasons and the changes they bring. Christmas time has always been a favorite for him as long as I can remember.

Connecting with Leroy on a personal level in making this book project come to life has been a rewarding and inspiring experience. We are ever grateful for having the opportunity to work with Leroy as he submits articles for PCBE. His connection to the Anabaptist communities have taken him across the country a few times. After discussing his venture to travel into the unknown, Leroy decided to take the plunge. He and his nephew Jeffery embarked on a 37-day adventure to travel to 13 countries! Once during their travels, Leroy called while he was drinking his morning coffee and we were drinking our evening tea. The great difference in the time zones, we found interesting. The language barrier throughout the trip proved to be trying, but the experience was fun for them. He even thought that he may learn a few new languages.

A few days into his trip he called (from Indonesia) and asked if we would pray for him; he had gotten very sick from a mosquito bite and their travels were delayed for 5 days. We were thankful for a full recovery!

A fresh cup of coffee, sometimes (Luwak), over a good 10,000-piece puzzle is the best way to get a good story from him; invite him over and you will be well entertained! He says puzzles are a good way to relax the brain at the end of the day.

His passion for the poor people he met throughout their journey was very thought provoking and sobering. He mentions the man without legs pushing a cart down the street as a memory he will never forget. Also, people living in tents without clean water. "We have so much to be thankful for," he remarks. Travel beside him throughout this book and you will find many interesting places and facts about countries we may never have the opportunity to see.

Let us always remember to give thanks in all and glory to God.

~John Lapp, the author's colleague

Watching a small black Audi with tinted windows turning into the driveway one Saturday in early March 2017 made me a bit nervous and apprehensive. Several days prior, we spoke on the phone for the first time and had discussed a potential job opening at PCBE, and now I was about to meet Leroy Martin at a neutral location for the first time, at a residence in New Holland, PA where the two of us had planned to meet and go to Yoder's Restaurant for lunch. No, we did not meet at a neutral location due to security concerns!

After a yummy lunch at Yoder's and after a lengthy chat, I felt as if I had made a new friend and was excited to offer Leroy a new job and see what his creativity will bring onboard.

2 ½ years have already elapsed since that cold wintry day and I am very glad that our lives crossed paths, I feel as if Leroy has taught me lots of things along the way and it has been an interesting journey thus far. Discussing and planning future trips has always been interesting. Being the poet that he is has brought many a smile to my face.

I feel privileged to be able to learn first-hand from Leroy of the many diverse cultures that can be found within all the different communities in the USA, and even across the world. Leroy has met some unique characters and hearing firsthand accounts of all the special places he has visited along the way and seeing the photos from some of his travel experiences has really broadened my horizons. My hope is that by the time you reach the last chapter in this book, your horizons will be less narrow than when you started.

~Raymond Lapp, publisher of Plain Communities Business Exchange

Leroy and I have gotten to known each other well over the years and more so as he became my neighbor and farming assistant for the past few years. He went from being a steel worker to a globe trotter and author in short order. In a conversation with Leroy, he told me that while working as a steel building erector, some of the projects he worked on were in proximity of the Newark International Airport. While observing the international flights coming and going, a deep longing would rise from his heart to be a passenger on one of the airplanes.

Here we hold a book that tells us that he was blessed to do so. We might do well to never let go of our dreams. Knowing Leroy, he always had a deep interest in people and their way of life. This is a firsthand account through the eyes of an Anabaptist taking us around the world through multiple Asian countries, South Korea, New Zealand and to the United Arab Emirates.

The boys thought I should see them off to Asia, so I said sure. I then made the necessary return arrangements as they were giving me a one-way trip to the airport. One fine morning we met Leroy's nephew Jeffery at Leroy's office. Leroy arranged his final things, then we piled in Jeffery's rental car and headed for the Newark International Airport. Having met Jeffery for the first time, gave me the impression that he is quiet and a little nervous and more so as we approached the airport entrance. It was understandable as it was his first time navigating the entrance into a busy airport, flying commercially and traveling abroad.

After dropping the car at the rental agency, we took the air-tram to the correct terminal. After printing their tickets and checking their luggage, we headed for the tunnel that took them out to the correct gates. Here is where we parted ways, as boarding passes were needed to go beyond this point. It was disappointing, as I had been wanting to see them board the plane. After a hearty handshake and goodbye, I wished them a safe journey before they disappeared from sight. Moments later, I found a good spot where I could watch air traffic come and go.

Did I feel I might not see Leroy again? It really did not cross my mind. Knowing Leroy's random ways of doing things, he has a way of navigating around obstacles that amazes me. I have come to a place where I expect the unexpected. After meeting Leroy some 5 weeks later, he had the biggest smile possible. I took it that the Asian folks had taught him something. It got me thinking I need to meet these people as well.

While reading this book, I found it very interesting to learn of the many ways in which people make their living who have a lot less than we Americans. Floating farm markets on the Mekong River, where the buyer and seller would conduct their transactions from their small boats. Repairing garments while sitting at a sewing machine beside the road. Using hand cranked, smoky generators to make espressos, and training camels for racing in the Dubai desert, is naming a few. Speaking of camel racing takes us to the glistening city of Dubai where we ride the elevator to the top of the world's tallest building. The excessive lifestyles the Dubai city offers the rich tourists is a stark contrast from the poor people in Southeast Asia. We learn that, despite the struggles of the poor to make a living, they still have a smile to share with a stranger. I find that there is much to learn from other humans around the world and lest we forget, let's remember that God created every one of them.

~Lavern Martin

It is a very interesting and adventurous journey my friend Leroy and his nephew Jeffrey took. Leroy gives us a glimpse how people live, from the poorest, to the richest, and how people treated them along the way.

I had the privilege to travel by train, to Newark Liberty International Airport to meet them as they flew home from the country of Dubai. I was excited when Leroy told me I could come welcome them back to the United States after they had been traveling for nearly six weeks. Never having been to an airport before, I was a little anxious that I would be able to find them. Thankfully, I found the right terminal. Interestingly, I could watch people from different countries arrive, greeting friends and family that were waiting for their loved ones. After waiting about an hour, I finally saw my friends' weary, but smiling faces. I could not imagine how it felt to travel all those thousands of miles and finally be so close to home. To me they seemed tired but satisfied that the stress and lag of the journey had been worth it. I had to smile when I remembered that one of the first things Leroy did was treat Jeffrey and I to some coffee and cinnamon rolls, as we sat around a table and talked. Thank you, Leroy, for sharing your stories with me and many others. I am quite certain you inspired many people along your journey as well as your friends back home.

~Wilson Martin

I was so amazed to hear that someone actually had the opportunity to travel around the world in thirty-seven days. How amazing what our dear Savior plans for us.

It was also so surprising to read that rice can be prepared in more than a hundred different ways. I also took notice on how it said that a woman was worshipping in the middle of the street; I can't imagine.

I was really pleased with your book. It is awesome.

May God bless you.

~A reader, Sharon Louise, age 13

I found your book very interesting. I really enjoyed reading it. It reminded me that I should be thankful for what I have. I would definitely recommend this book to other people. Thanks for putting it together.

~Becky M. Peachey, grade seven

I really liked your book, Leroy. What I liked best was how they make coffee and the Japanese bullet trains. I really think you should make this book because I found it very interesting. Thanks for sharing the book.

~Ivan Lee King Jr., grade eight

It was very interesting to see how other countries do their things. What interested me the most was how they make that coffee or the speed of the bullet trains in Japan. Very interesting book.

~DJ King, grade eight

INTRODUCTION

Why do we travel?

Seemingly since the dawn of day, humans have enjoyed exploring the diversities of life which consist outside their own geographical borders. The annals of history contain many accounts of humans traveling on their own volition, far beyond what was considered their homelands. Throughout the centuries, primary modes of transportation have unequivocally transformed our methods of traveling, enabling us to cover vast distances within increasingly shorter time frames. Perhaps the era in which the greater part of these changes took place is between 1850 to 1950.

Traveling is expensive and time consuming, even if done by a budget-conscious person. Traveling—especially internationally—is also quite tiring and lonely and can leave you wishing that you hadn't ever left the friendly confines and warm cocoon-like spaces of your home. Additionally, traveling can unexpectedly fill your heart and expand your mind and worldview by observing the spectacular variety of people groups whom God has created.

As the author of this book, it is my desire that you, the reader, will perhaps gain a fresh insight of how some people, other than ourselves, live their day-to-day lives. When I began working for Plain Communities Business Exchange, I could not have imagined traveling alone to far-off countries. To be clear, that was never the actual assignment, either. Permit me to explain briefly. While working for PCBE, domestic travel quickly became a part of the normal routine for me, as I traveled throughout a host of Plain communities with the purpose and intent of interviewing Plain business owners and farmers. I would listen intently to these inspiring individuals' life stories. I would then, upon the conclusion of the interviews, go back to my office and document the interview in a written story form, which would be printed sometime later within our business magazine.

Throughout this line of work, I became increasingly fascinated with people and the unique challenges they had faced and were able to overcome. In some of these instances, incredible and seemingly insurmountable obstacles had been wrestled effectively. I began to wonder what other people's lives across the vast globe consisted of. Having always been interested in humans and their behavior patterns, beliefs, fears, hopes, and dreams, I explained to my employer Raymond that I would relish the opportunity to travel internationally to Europe during the winter of 2017-2018. Thankfully, he did not forbid me to explore a greater part of our world. It was on this trip, while traveling solo for more than five weeks, that my previously narrow worldview began to expand a wee bit.

Upon returning from visiting twenty-six countries in Europe, not much time had elapsed before I experienced a longing to visit the poorer regions throughout Asia. My nephew Jeffrey had mentioned, shortly after the conclusion of my European travels, that he would like to accompany me on my next international journey, if I ever decided to embark on another.

Initially, when I mentioned that my next trip would very likely consist of the Asian territories, he became disinterested—until I disclosed the fact that I would also be traveling to Australia and New Zealand. No sooner had this news reached his ears, that Jeffrey concluded that he would be interested in accompanying me on my journey after all.

He and I learned so many valuable lessons on this recent Asian journey of ours, that we both consider it to have been a monumental moment in our lives. We met scores of generous, friendly people within the poorest of regions. I remember returning home to America feeling guilty for having left so many of my newly formed friendships behind. The trip impacted me in more ways than I had conceivably imagined possible.

Why do we write books?

It is widely known that the printing of books increased prolifically immediately after Johannes Gutenberg's invention of movable type. The introduction of such an incredible technology around 1450 (AD) greatly facilitated the dissemination of written literature throughout Europe and beyond. According to many literary professors, books and various forms of written literature spread like wildfire following the introduction of movable type. The printing press is also believed to have been directly responsible for aiding the prolific spread of religious literature immediately before and during the Reformation, which began in the early 1500s.

Centuries later, the process and applications of printing presses and the appearance of books have changed dramatically. Even though more than one million new books are printed each year, various factors and elements are threatening the very future of the physical book. A growing number of luminaries and literary professors warn that within a couple generations, people may not even know what books were or are— at least not physical literature. These folks expect the landscape of the printing industries to undergo a complete transformation within a few decades.

It is expected that books will eventually be available in digital forms only. Even today, regardless if the words are in digital form or appear in hardcopy, the word *book* is used to describe every element of it, including the paper, glue, words, binding, etc.

At the incipience of this introduction, I had raised a few questions. It is not possible that one man could speak for every writer or for every traveler, so in this regard, I will perhaps attempt to explain only why I have written this book and why I travel. However, I doubt that my observations stray far from the worn path occupied by scores of travel writers who have blazed the literary trail before me.

Perhaps we write books to share real accounts and stories with people whom might never be presented with an opportunity to explore the countries and people groups around them. Perhaps we travel to escape—if only for a short while—our all-too-familiar lives. Perhaps that is why we read books in the first place—to be transported—albeit briefly—into another time and place without leaving our familiarities too far behind. In conclusion, perhaps we travel, read, and write books to gain more sense of our world, enabling us to extrapolate with greater clarity and discernment, and to make the world around us appear smaller and our differences more manageable and understandable.

~*Leroy Martin*

CHAPTER 1
FIGHTING FATIGUE ON ULTRA-MARATHON FLIGHTS

Nothing could prepare me for all that I was about to witness. Sure, I could immerse my mind in a thousand books composed by great travel writers. Or listen to a hundred lectures from a sea of articulate orators. If that all failed, I could certainly watch endless hours of slides and videos teaching of cultural disparity. However, none of these platforms would ever truly be adequate in preparing the eyes and mind of a pampered, sheltered American. At least, not for me. It simply had to be seen with my own eyes for any of it to have made any sense.

My travel partner and nephew Jeffrey Martin and I were told by several well-meaning individuals that traveling across dozens of time zones will be exhausting. They did not lie. It was. But if we were to break through the travel weary haze which was so intense it seemed to occasionally hinder our eyesight, and if we were completely honest with ourselves, we would tell you it was all worth it. Because it really was.

I am unsure where to start with this story. It seems a bit overwhelming to begin describing our experiences within the thirteen countries which we toured throughout thirty-seven days. Sometimes it felt as if we were trapped inside the middle of a swirling whirlwind. We saw so much that at times, it was discouraging and inspiring, all within a matter of a few seconds.

But every story must have a beginning and an ending, and I suppose I shouldn't break from the ranks of storytelling now by starting this journey with the conclusion. So, in chronological order, I will attempt to share some of the highlights from our 45,693-mile journey across the globe.

Every great adventure usually begins with an idea and a plan. Well, sort of. Some people's plans are much more thought-out than others. But not mine—at least not always. Especially not when I am on vacation. Bear in mind and realize that I embrace spontaneity as my middle name when I travel. I have discovered that it makes for a much more memorable journey. Seriously, I haven't yet met anyone who proudly proclaimed how his or her perfectly obsessive itinerary permitted them to have an entirely random, unforgettable experience while journeying to unfamiliar continents. In my feeble opinion, it is best to remain flexible and malleable while traveling, in much the same way as a Vietnamese motorbike driver deftly navigates the harrowing streets of Ho Chi Minh City.

Motorbikes in Ho Chi Minh, Vietnam compete for space in a crowded city street

On a clear morning in late February 2019, I bid farewell to my friends and family, without a guarantee that I would ever see them again. The unfamiliar had come calling at my door again, beckoning me to follow, at least for a few short weeks. Of course, I felt obliged to heed such an urgent call, and had eagerly packed my luggage in anticipation of a wonderful learning journey of the earth that God created and the people He loves so dearly and cherishes so unconditionally.

Jeffrey and I waved goodbye one final time to our friend Lavern Martin before we hurriedly marched toward the departure terminal at Newark Liberty International. We had managed to pass through security with a breeze, not knowing at that point in time that we would be subjected to invasive security scanners twenty-six additional times before we stepped foot on American soil again. Endless lines at international airports throughout the world is not something that interests me, nor you, so I will skip right on to more engaging topics.

The Asian country of Singapore was the first on our global to-see list. But first, we were required to survive being cramped inside an airplane for a total of twenty-three and-a-half hours. As we soared to heights which exceeded thirty-seven-thousand feet, I glanced curiously at the electronic

Singapore's financial district pierces the city skyline

display panel on the back of my seat. The outside temperature was minus seventy-one degrees Fahrenheit, according to the airplane's thermometer readings. I guess it wasn't so bad to be relaxing, albeit fitfully, within the crowded confines of our aircraft after all. I would rather be crowded and warm any day than freeze to death within mere seconds.

Thanks to the excellent work of the aircraft crew, our big bird touched down safely on the Singapore tarmac at the scheduled time. Having slept very little during the nearly twenty-four-hour marathon flight, we completed disembarkation and signed the required immigration documents upon arrival. We passed through immigration booths which captured our biometric information, including our fingerprints and our iris prints. As soon as that intimidating chore was completed, we were free to explore our first country as we pleased.

Streams of water flow from the mouth of a celebrated monument

Having to deal with a twelve-hour time change, we felt less than our best selves, to be sure. It seemed as if we literally skipped right through an entire twelve hours, like they had never been there at all. The clock indicated that we were now twelve hours ahead of our American counterparts on the east coast. Even though it was dark when we left the airport in California, (where our flight had a layover) it remained dark for a total of no less than nineteen hours as our aircraft pierced the skies. It was, figuratively and literally, the longest night of my life.

Later that day, with our travel weary heads reeling from misery, and not knowing the difference between night and day, we crashed out on the beds at four in the afternoon and slept away most of our jet lag till the first streaks of light painted the Asian skies. The following morning, we

A United Airlines plane awaits on the tarmac at San Francisco International

Our initial introduction to Asian cuisine

gingerly marched our trembling American stomachs to the nearby food stalls and introduced them to Asian cuisine. They weren't initially impressed. It was still early morning but most of the stalls were open along the streets, which had come alive with the song of a thousand motorbikes drumming the chipped asphalt as motorists competed like soldiers in opposing armies as they nudged for a few inches of space while making their way to work.

Before we travel on through the continent to Thailand, I will share a few numbers with you in the following paragraph, so that you can grasp a greater understanding of our undertaking while we were so far away from the tranquil fields of Lancaster County for nearly six weeks.

Throughout the duration of our trek across two continents and thirteen countries, we primarily traveled via aircraft. Jeffrey and I logged a total of 102 hours and 30 minutes

The second meal in Asia (squid is peculiar looking)

in the air to get to our various destinations. We also spent 30 minutes clinging to the broad back of a lumbering elephant as the mighty animal barreled through the jungles of Thailand.

The author (with hat) and his nephew Jeffrey

There were several other unique methods of transportation which we experienced, as well. For nearly twenty minutes, we were entertained while perched precariously on camels which transported us briefly through the Arabian Desert. A whopping sixty hours whittled away as we sat in taxi cabs or privately hired cars throughout our journey. Not to be completely outdone, several boats also had the opportunity of charming us as they took us to see floating villages and floating markets, as well as gliding effortlessly past several hundred islands in a single day. A total of sixteen hours disappeared quickly after we boarded the boats and, in most situations, we had been passengers who were told that life jackets aren't important to wear throughout the duration of the journeys. "You must only wear when water is choppy," the captains remarked in an equally choppy Asian accent.

We had the opportunity to be esteemed guests on a desert excursion while riding in a 1961 Land Rover. The vehicle was open-air, no windows, and I managed to get sand in my teeth and various other annoying places before the day was done. After three-and-a-half hours perusing through the bumpy sand dunes, we called it quits.

Last, but certainly not least, the Shinkansen bullet train system in Japan also deserves an honorable mention. Speaking of honor, I will expound on the Japanese honor system in a later chapter of this book. I cherished every hour that went by while on the bullet trains. To whiz by at such impressive speeds of 191 mph—on the ground—is rather fascinating, I think. A knowledgeable friend of mine told me that even airplanes generally don't travel that fast before takeoff. I don't know if my friend's statement is accurate, but I do know that I was truly appreciative of the fact that we never "took off" while hurtling at lightning speeds across the Japanese landscape in their ever-impressive bullet trains.

A Japanese bullet train arrives at a station

So, now that you are familiar with our various modes of transportation, perhaps I can divulge some more details as to where we all traveled to during our nearly-six-week stint. The following countries, though not necessarily in any particular order, are as follows. Singapore, Thailand, Malaysia, Indonesia, Australia, New Zealand, Laos, Cambodia, Vietnam, Hong Kong, Dubai, Japan, South Korea, and the Australia-ruled island of Tasmania. We will certainly discuss the friendly Christian community who practices communal living and at present, resides on the island of Tasmania.

To travel this great of a distance—more than 45,000-miles—requires a lot of fuel for the aircraft as well as for the human spirit. Jeff and I tried to travel really fast for the first few weeks, in efforts to continually stay ahead of the initial jet lag that we were told takes some people weeks to get over. So, our initial game plan was; outrun the jet lag before it can catch up with us. But it did catch up eventually, and in a very big and nasty way.

Colors reflect in the pools close to Singapore's famed Orchard Road

Unfortunately, I fell gravely ill in Indonesia for several days and wasn't quite sure the exact cause of it, although I suspect a mosquito bite is the culprit. A pesky little insect had bit me and caused a sizable welt to form on my arm. About a day later I began to exhibit classic signs of Dengue Fever, which some mosquitoes can carry in the sub-tropical region of Indonesia.

Of course, I had nervously been self-diagnosing, and it is never flattering to self-diagnose even in your home country, much less a foreign country 10,200 miles from your home. I am extremely grateful for the prayers of several of my dear friends and family members as they offered up urgent prayers for my speedy recovery. Their requests were answered, and within

Towering buildings twinkle in the sultry night skies

five days I began to feel happy and human again.

I will share a few more statistics with you before we go any further. We occupied twenty-one flights and passed through security scanners twenty-seven times, as mentioned previously. The greatest time difference between the east coast of the United States and where we traveled

A tourist photographs one of Singapore's most iconic buildings

to later in the trip was eighteen hours, while we visited New Zealand. We were able to call home and tell our friends and family that we are experiencing a gorgeous Wednesday morning while they were still stuck with dealing with the pressures and struggles of Tuesday, etc. Several times, we were eating our breakfast while back home in America, they were only eating their dinners from our previous day. It was kind of fun, this vast difference in our time zones.

If you choose to follow along from the comfort of your armchairs, Jeffrey and I will take you on a journey of more exciting countries as we explore unique cultural traits and habits. Having traveled to the richest city in the world as well as some of the poorest regions on the globe, the stark dichotomy of excessive wealth and staggering poverty was nearly incomprehensible on several occasions.

CHAPTER 2
BIG CATS AND FAST RIDES

The roar of the noisy engines from the antiquated boats filled the stagnant air around the tourist-infested island in Thailand. Jeffrey and I had arrived just in the nick of time. We had slept longer than most self-respecting tourists should and had been scrambling the rest of the morning with our itinerary. Making up for lost time is no fun, although some of us—perhaps you can personally relate—have turned a habitually late lifestyle into an art. Let's hope not.

Gliding across the shimmering bays of Phucket

Beautiful boats can be spotted as they enter and egress the dozens of busy bays

We woke up with a desire to see pristine beaches and to gaze into a perpetually shimmering abyss of clear waters. Well, at least we got half of what we longed for. Rushing to the door of the small tourist shack which displayed photographs of perfect beaches and islands, we pushed open the door and

A boat is docked at a bay

announced that we wished to be taken on a tour of said scenery.

Apparently, the people of Thailand are early risers, because the lady behind the desk informed us that we have mere minutes to catch the boat, which was located a short distance away. She promised us that if we would immediately pay for the tour, she would ensure us passage on a guided boat tour. At this point we were rather reluctant, because the boat supposedly would leave the dock at 10 AM sharp, and we were a good twenty-minute taxi drive from that location and the local time was 9:50 AM. Needless to say, everything in the universe would be required to align perfectly if we were to reach our boat in time. Even so, it looked as if that might be a stretch.

As the situation developed and we had hurriedly paid the kind lady for the tour, we were escorted to a taxi where the driver was given specific instructions in the Thai language. The lady must have told him to drive like a madman, because that is exactly what took place for the next twenty minutes. I remember being scared and thinking to myself, 'ok, this was silly, we could have just waited to take this tour another day if the driver has no intentions of getting us there alive anyway.'

But all my Americanized *(is that a word?)* fretting had been in vain. Our taxi driver was obviously an expert at navigating the traffic-laden country roads of his hometown with the ease and finesse of a stock car driver. He probably honed his incredible driving skills through years of transporting late, sleepy tourists to this exact location hundreds if not thousands of times. Just when I thought things couldn't get much more dangerous for us, traffic-wise, our frazzled yet

A monk, while on an early morning stroll, shares the streets with motorbikes

apparently quite skilled driver retrieves his cell phone from his pocket and proceeds to make a call while narrowly escaping an impact with a slow-moving vegetable wagon maneuvering toward the nearby roadside market.

After holding an increasingly escalated conversation in Thai, he shoved the phone back in his pocket and turned to face us, smiling reassuring. "Everything is ok. We will be on time. The boat, it will wait for you," he shared, beaming proudly. Jeffery and I nearly beamed proudly as well, because it was rather impressive the strings that our taxi driver had obviously just pulled on our behalf.

Majestic limestone monoliths grace the memorable Phang Nga Bay

Talk about an excellent business model. Halfway around the world, here in a region of Thailand where most roads were unpaved, Jeffery and I were the only thing that seemed to matter to our driver. It was evident that we, his customers, were his top priority at the time. We had become his main objective and ultimate responsibility. This kind gentleman cared so much whether we arrived at our boat on time, that he went out of his way to call ahead to the boat crew to inform them that he is transporting two eager American boys— and probably that they should clear the area of pedestrians because his car is coming in hot and the possibility of the vehicle drifting was real and not just imagined.

At any rate, we did arrive safely, with all four wheels on the dusty ground when we approached the boat launch area. I was a bit ashamed of myself, to think that I had been initially reluctant to pay for the tour, because the office hadn't looked 'professional enough' and my *scam alert* began sending off all kinds of signals. But here was a testimony of typical Thai hospitality. Our driver could have just as easily driven through the streets at a leisurely pace with no care in the world, instead of putting his and our lives at risk by driving aggressively just so that we wouldn't be late for our non-refundable tour which he was in no way responsible to reimburse if we missed the boat.

Playing games with the clock wasn't always going to work in our favor on this trip, though, as we were about to discover in a few weeks from today. Little did we know that our punctuality, or lack thereof, would be sorely tried and tested in the delightfully yet obsessively punctual country of Japan. But that is a story for another chapter, right now we have a boat which you and I need to catch!

Catching a few winks before the next wave of tourists floods his watercraft

So far, we discussed quite a few statistics and numbers regarding the international trip I was on. In this chapter, we will keep some interesting statistics at bay—literally—as we glide down various bays in the southern regions of picturesque Thailand. The water won't be sparkling, though, so try to mask your disappointment and the stench of the soiled waters by grabbing a fabric mask to cover your nose. I did not but should have. Nonetheless, I survived, and my nasal passages are at present, not much worse for the wear.

With considerable fanfair, the evening sky provided a most visceral experience

While here in the considerably hospitable country of Thailand, we visited Loh Lana Bay, Phang Nga Bay, the Phi Phi Islands, and Banana Beach. The scenery was quite intriguing as you might imagine. Hundreds of tiny islands appeared and then disappeared from our view as our colorful boat glided past on the green-hued waters. The weather was quite warm and humid, typical for the summertime in the sub-tropical region.

A highlight of the nine-hour journey was when the boat operator docked at a well-known island for approximately forty minutes. This allowed us ample time to splash through the shallow waters and walk barefooted through the sandy beach area. We were not alone though. Police officers in military fatigues patrolled the small island—their watchful gaze was never averted and was seemingly trained on us for the duration of the short visit.

James Bond Island, perhaps the most-visited spot in the whole of Thailand

Around mid-day, after some of the reveling had dissipated, we were treated to a wonderfully authentic Thai meal. From the various countries which we broke bread in—or more aptly—struggled with chopsticks, I must say Japan and Thailand served the most amazing food and spices. It is true, rice can be beautifully prepared in more than one-hundred different ways, however, at the end of the day, it is still rice. And by the end of our six-week journey, we were quite ready to trade in our chopsticks and sticky rice for a hands-on, greasy, American burger again. You can take the boy out of the country, but you can't easily take the hunger for all-beef patties out of the boy.

A pineapple infused with rice and chicken curiously sates the appetite

So, there we were, clutching our chopsticks like unfamiliar Americans, attempting to carefully navigate and master the tricky travel distance from plate to mouth. Until one gets better acquainted with the unusual eating utensils, I believe you could suffice it to say that we worked hard for our meals sometimes, because each time the food fell off the chopsticks en route to our mouth, we needed to try all over again. Even though the food is quite tasty, it can feel like

Giving the chopsticks a run for their money

Indecipherable condiments on a Thai table hint of the usual suspects

a losing battle when it is 105 degrees Fahrenheit and you are on a rocking boat which is itself simultaneously occupied with cresting the small waves of the shore.

Another highlight for Jeffrey was when the boat operator permitted him to take control of the vessel for a few minutes. There he was, an American farm boy, manning a watercraft while transporting more than two dozen human lives, all while navigating the many islands within the Thailand bays. Profound moments like these are certainly difficult to erase from one's memory bank.

The day passed by all too quickly, and before we knew it, the puffy white clouds and blue skies were being aggressively replaced by the colorful hues of the night sky. Our boat reached the final destination shortly before nightfall and upon exiting the watercraft, we climbed in a minivan and endured yet another frenzied ride through heavy traffic. This country at least had adequate road signage within its city limits; we visited several countries that lacked all road signage and stoplights within their cities, which makes for very interesting travels, trust me. It does seem as if our home country has excessive amounts of highway regulations, however; I think it is a good thing. Even so, the Asian drivers seemed to understand the rules of the road quite well without signage in several regions of Laos, Cambodia, and Vietnam, which we will get to later.

Small fishing boats sway upon the waters as gentle waves persist

Several other adventures were born into existence here in Thailand. If you would think that I possessed the common sense to stay out of a cage filled with five adult tigers— yes, live ones—I would tell you that you are sadly mistaken. Some heavy convincing was

Tranquil scenes such as these are evocative of island nations

A tiger sits patiently while a trainer instructs

required, but I managed to convince Jeffrey, the wiser of us two, that my idea wasn't the worst ever. He reluctantly agreed to join me as we delicately walked through the door into the tiger den. I distinctly remember thinking, "I hope I won't regret this."

It was quite creepy to walk stealthily into the lair of a wild animal's unnatural habitat, hoping that the beasts would be so kind as to refrain from snacking on us. Several trainers accompanied us, wielding large bamboo sticks. (As if that will stop an aggressive tiger from attacking anyone).

Everything went well though, and only once throughout the fifteen minutes spent inside the cage did the trainer need to tell me to move around more slowly if I wished to avoid startling the big cats. Well, of course I wished very much to avoid that, so I consciously moved *much* slower until I was standing safely on the other side of the cage. The single reason we went to live on the edge like this was at the behest of our taxi driver. "You should go there," he ventured. When we hesitated for a bit he followed with a "You must. Everyone from America likes it." Well then, with those words, it had been settled.

You might be interested in knowing the animals were very likely tranquilized, although I have no proof of that. I do, however, happen to know that the majestic and lethal cats were not declawed, as I had been so sure they would be, prior to my entrance into the cage.

"Are the animals declawed?" I inquired deliberately, directing my question at the trainer who could speak English the best.

"Come here, let me show you," he excitedly remarked. He marched me right up to one of the larger cats, mere inches from its mouth, and bent down to pick up one of its paws. As the trainer pressed down slightly on the soft, padded flesh on the bottom of its paw with his shoes, my fears were revealed. The cats were not declawed. Sharp, pointy needle-like claws shot out from under the padded feet of the tiger. Immediately I took one look at

A petro station in Thailand

The light of day surrenders beautifully to a persistent kaleidoscope of colors

Jeffrey and declared, "It is time we get out of here." He did not disagree and in his haste, nearly beat me to the door.

CHAPTER 3
LUWAK COFFEE FARMS AND LUMBERING ELEPHANTS

The days are lengthy for a young elephant as it stands chained between tour rides

Crashing through the jungles of Thailand on the back of an adult elephant who is busy navigating through banana groves and coconut trees while you are simultaneously swatting away pesky mosquitoes and other unfamiliar insects is exactly what it sounds like. Busy and exciting. Throughout the ride, the elephant handler explained a few details of the large animal's habits and eating preferences. Upon the conclusion of our little expedition, the elephant was cooled down with a water hose, refreshing him from the intense rays of the beating summer sun. I thought it would also have been nice to be offered a respite from the sweltering journey, and briefly considered asking the handler if the riders could also receive a cool, watery break. Deciding against it, I instead grabbed for my handkerchief and wiped heavy beads of sweat from my forehead. It was, after all, winter back in the United States, and my friends and coworkers were probably wishing they could trade the piles of snow and ice for a sultry day once again.

As you might expect, elephants are not the most elegant creatures, and can appear exceptionally clumsy, especially when they begin walking. According to an article which appeared recently in the journal *Nature,* most elephants can reach top speeds of ten and fifteen miles per hour when they run. If you think about it, it might not be as slow as you would initially imagine, especially when all that weight comes rushing at you at such a rate of speed.

I certainly didn't expect an elephant's hide or skin to be soft like a baby's, however; I also didn't necessarily expect it to be as coarse as it was. The hide was terribly rough to the touch—it almost hurt when I ran my hands across the back of the large brute. They are kind creatures though, and almost seemed playful as they transported us through the jungles. According to scientists, elephants are some of the few animals who possess self-perception. For example, in a recent study, when trainers applied a large blot of paint to the side of an elephant's body and then placed a full-body mirror in front of the animal, the elephant continually extended its trunk, urgently attempting to remove the spot of paint from its body, knowing that it doesn't belong there.

Now that our ride has concluded, with a complimentary banana—for us, not the elephant—we will catch a short flight and head to Malaysia, home of the iconic Petronas Towers. The country has a high concentration of Muslims, and upon our arrival

A sign spotted in inner city Kuala Lumpur

at the airport, we were transported to our hotel in a taxi driven by a Muslim woman who had covered most of her face with a hijab. The head covering is symbolic to women of the Islamic faith, in much the same way as a head covering is important to Anabaptist Christian women. The hijab, however, features a much-higher concentration of coverage when compared to a small veil or prayer cap popular in Anabaptist circles. It is customary to wear these hijabs, even if the woman works at

Pockets of squalor and stark poverty, while still prevalent, are nearly squeezed in a death grip as the city's richest continue their expansion

McDonalds. During our stay in Malaysia, we walked into a McDonalds where five smiling Muslim women had covered their heads with coverings. They greeted us warmly. It certainly was a unique cultural experience for two American boys.

A typical Malaysian breakfast consists of baked beans and assorted fruits

We arrived in the country shortly after midnight, so there was not much for us to see as our car hurtled down the highway for seventy minutes under the cloak of darkness. The airport was located far from Kuala Lumpur, and as we finally arrived at the city limits, the Petronas Towers, lit up like two glittering spires, proudly welcomed us to the city.

Later the following morning, with the sun hotter than ever, or so it seemed, we explored much of the city on foot. It was here in this country that I observed something which I considered to be rather exceptional. Now, I know that the poor and homeless are among us in the United States, especially in large cities, but here in Kuala Lumpur, the capital city of Malaysia, it was surprising to see rudimental shacks (homes) constructed of rusty tin, rotting wood, and torn plastic, all

The lights of the iconic Petronas Towers playfully wink throughout the night

Small living quarters occupy the shadows which are cast by looming structures of Malaysia's hoteliers and financial institutions

directly resting in the shadows of looming financial monuments which threatened to boldly reach past the clouds.

These exquisite, shimmering skyscrapers emblazoned with the names of global banks simply were placed right in the middle of what appeared to be a community of squalor. That might sound like a harsh description, but if you would have accompanied Jeffrey and I on a ninety-minute walk around the decrepit neighborhood, I am convinced that you would agree with my description. I guess all the money that flows through the dozens of central banks which we saw there simply didn't reach even a short five-minute walk outside their doors.

It was also in Malaysia that we witnessed another unusual sight, but this next one was considerably unsettling and caused a sense of dread to wash over us. While we were in line at the immigration booth awaiting our exit stamp out of the country, a distinct rattling rang loudly through

Inconceivably impoverished residences are sprinkled throughout the city

the corridors. The sound of heavy chains rattling grew louder, so I turned around to see whatever could be causing such a disturbance in the otherwise solemnly quiet hall.

What my eyes saw next startled me. A band of heavily armed police officers were escorting a group of approximately eight prisoners, shackled hand and foot by heavy chains. When the procession stopped just mere feet from us, the prisoners and I made eye contact. Most of them had haughty looks in their eyes and appeared considerably unrepentant and unashamed of their plight. Several of them were copiously tattooed and sported more steel (piercings) on their faces than you could shake a stick at. Some were even laughing in a menacing manner.

Burgers are sold here from this stand which sets along the congested streets

Pretending not to be scared by the situation which was enfolding, I quickly put on a brave face and averted my gaze. Glancing back several moments later, I couldn't believe what was happening. The prisoners were being released, one by one, and their chains, which had been tethering them safely to each other, fell to the ground. It was at that moment that I sincerely hoped that they would not be boarding the same aircraft that I would be occupying. Apparently, the chains had been released so that every individual could pass separately through immigration, of course, under the very watchful guise of the officers.

A few short hours after that pulse-quickening experience, we arrived safely in the beautiful yet incredibly humid country of Indonesia. (The prisoners did not occupy the same aircraft as ours).

Unparalleled hospitality is a distinct trademark here in Indonesia, in fact so much so that it was difficult for us to trust the natives, because to us brash Americans, these unwaveringly kind people were up to something nefarious. It took about three days for us to realize that kindness is a treasured virtue here, and so were the thousands of temples which scattered the countryside and occupied much of the city space.

It was close to 1 AM when we stepped off the plane in Denpasar, Bali. The sweltering humidity, even at that hour of the night, seemed to envelop us and hold our weak respiratory systems hostage. It was, I found, quite difficult to breathe freely in such a humid climate. Throughout the four day stay, my lungs hurt continually from the excessive humidity and the thick, blanketed haze of smog and emissions from the thousands of motorbikes and taxis which careened through the narrow alleys and streets.

Not everyone waits for the streetlight to change prior to crossing

Traffic here was perhaps the wildest we saw on our journey. Motorbikes were burdened with impressive loads of materials and products which their operators were transporting to various marketplaces and seemed to take precedent throughout the day as well as the night. It appeared as if each motoring entrepreneur attempted to outdo his fellow citizens by stacking more products on his motorbike than what seemed humanly possible to transport safely. These people could surely teach us American Amish and Mennonites how to be more efficient, that is for sure.

Early one morning, as our private taxi was motoring down the busy streets, we came upon an elderly woman who, at least to my American eyes, seemed distraught and in peril. She was, by all practical appearances, stranded in the middle of the street which was brimming with whirring traffic. The elderly woman was down on her hands and knees, and it appeared as if she was searching for something while dozens of motorbikes and cars whipped past her.

Breakfast in Indonesia is anything but boring when this guy keeps you company mere inches from your table

Towering high above the rest of the city structures, a mosque in Kuala Lumpur

Concerned for the woman's safety—even her life—my American mind went into overdrive. "What is she looking for?" I loudly asked our driver. Not waiting for his response, I added quickly, "We must stop and help her. She will get hit!"

An intriguing and familiar octagon shape which is indicative of similar road rules practiced within the US

"No, she will not get hit," the driver replied matter-of-factly. And then answering my question, he replied simply, "She is worshipping. Everybody does this. Indonesian people go to pray to the Gods, sometimes in the middle of the streets, morning and evening. This is not unusual."

Well, that was an interesting cultural lesson. I had no idea that risking one's life to pray in the busy streets of Bali would be a respectable, religious activity. As we navigated safely past the kneeling elderly woman, I wondered how such a custom even began to take root. The scene was a rather interesting one to behold. Scores of motorists were simply maneuvering around this worshipping woman, not even blowing their horns in exasperation or even clipping her closely with their vehicles. It was indeed, a legitimate, recognized practice, since later that day we saw several more people praying in the middle of busy streets.

I had to ask myself, if this was a customary practice within Christianity, would I be willing to risk my life to pray in the middle of a narrow street which was bustling with frenzied amounts of traffic? Perhaps I would be, if the motorists were thoughtful.

Widi, our driver for two days, also explained why there is such an unbelievably high concentration of temples in this country. In certain areas where Hinduism is practiced, it is customary and honorable for every male to build a "family temple" upon marrying. I guess this would accurately explain why there were thousands of small and large temples erected

Temples such as this one are revered within Indonesian culture

throughout the countryside as well as the cities.

Some of the temples were decrepit and in gross disrepair, while many others had weathered the climate and the passing years quite well, remaining stalwart and steadied under the relentless, year-round sunshine and wind.

On several occasions we saw new temples being constructed throughout the area, since recently married Hindu men were building their family temples with the help of friends and family, wielding simple and basic tools. Nearly all the temples we saw were constructed by bricks, each temple prominently displaying figures of their various Gods. Sometimes these brick figures were shockingly grotesque and horribly disfigured, yet each represented a significant

Perhaps the most famous ancient structure in all of Indonesian

A Civet cat peers out from behind the confines of her captivity

and important part of the Hindu religion.

Although Indonesia is a multireligious country bordered by the Indian Ocean, the predominant religions here are Hinduism and Islam. The prevailing religion might differ in Jakarta, Bali, and Sumatra, all regions within Indonesia which feature diverse ethnicities. Muslims and Christians can be found here throughout Indonesia, but according to Widi, those groups are vastly in the minority.

During our stay in Indonesia, we toured a Luwak coffee farm. I was quite surprised to see dozens of small cages, each occupied by a specific species of wild cats, on these unique coffee farms. I was told by the farm managers that the cats are pertinent to the success of these coffee farms. He then asked if I wished to taste a fresh cup of designer coffee that was "refined" by the cat's digestive system.

It isn't Starbucks, but still quite drinkable

Laundry which hangs from the front porch of a city dweller, dries in the rays of the midday sun

CHAPTER 4
INDONESIAN RICE FARMS AND MENNONITE-THEMED ROADSIDE STANDS

Convincing signage is strategically placed by savvy farmers and business opportunists

Jeffrey and I sought refuge from the intensity of the Indonesian sun by making a brief stop at a coffee farm along the outskirts of Bali. Here, numerous coffee farms dotted the landscape, each boasting that they sell and produce genuine Luwak coffee. But for those of you who are, as of this moment, unfamiliar with the distinctly unique choice of beverage, you might be wondering what exactly this mysterious and potentially overhyped Luwak coffee is.

I will attempt to explain it in a solicitous manner. For those of you who are squeamish, I invite you to bypass the following four paragraphs and continue your reading from there. For the braver ones, you will probably never look at coffee the same way again. Sorry.

"Why do you drink coffee that is made from beans which you say are refined by specific cats?" I quizzed the farmer.

"Here in Bali, Luwak coffee is the best because it is made from

A cup of Luwak designer coffee emits a most pleasing aroma

Seeing yet ignoring the distraught look on my face, he continued right along with his presentation. "The cats then pass the beans whole, and we rummage through the excretion and collect them. The beans are thoroughly cleaned before the roasting and grinding process begins." He added, "Many farmers here in Indonesia have begun practicing this method of coffee production, since a global demand for this distinctly unique

Rudimentary residences provide little comfort for workers on the coffee farms

coffee beans that are harvested and collected from the excretion of Civet cats," he began. "You see, the cats greatly prefer to eat only the best coffee beans, they scrounge around for the premium beans and then swallow them whole. Once the beans are inside the cat's stomach, the acids within the cat's digestive system refines them, stripping the beans from any bitter aftertaste that is found in some coffees."

Cages which contain Civet cats can be found throughout the countryside

product has skyrocketed in the past several years, thanks to the Internet."

Coffee beans harvested from the excretion of Civet cats is certainly nothing new, however. The well-spoken farmer explained that when Indonesia and surrounding countries were subjected to Dutch rule, the Dutch became greedy and tried to harvest, consume, and sell as much coffee as they humanly could. This meant that there wasn't any

Coffee flowers bloom boldy in the warm tropical sun

Farmers are eager to sell the vegetative crops to anyone who passes by, haggling is both expected and respected

Flames sprout hungrily from the grill at a Hibachi restaurant in Indonesia

Jeffrey takes a turn at grinding coffee beans in a similar fashion as practiced many years ago

coffee left for the poor natives who actually performed all the hard work on the coffee farms for their rulers.

In time, the Indonesian farmers noticed that the cats who roamed around the coffee plantations were also caffeine fiends and were digesting the coffee beans and passing them whole. Desperate times call for desperate measures, so the farmers collected the previously consumed beans, washed them and roasted them. By doing this, the poorest, hardest working men and women here in Indonesia could still enjoy a cup of smooth, delectable coffee, even though the profit wary plantation owners had attempted to deny them the fruits of their labor. The point of the story is, I guess— try as you might— you simply can't get between a man and his coffee.

You might be wondering if Jeffrey and I were brave enough to sample such a cup of coffee that was brewed in such an unorthodox method?

Yes. Yes, we were, and it was amazingly smooth and refined, exactly as was promised and verbally advertised by the Indonesian coffee farmer. Of course, this specific coffee has been a wonderful crop for the farmers here, since it is extremely expensive and at present (2019), is being shipped worldwide.

Now that we have that out of the way, I sincerely hope that little coffee story didn't leave a bad taste in your mouth. I wanted to share that story with you because the persistence and diligence of the hardworking farmers from so many decades ago, had inspired me. It was, I felt, a testament to the human spirit. In even the most oppressive situations, all across the globe, there are still, to this very day, people who are surviving and managing on far less than you or I probably ever will.

It was also here in this country of exceptionally hospitable people, that I contracted a serious illness so grave that I was convinced that I might not see another

Demonstrating how coffee beans are roasted, a woman displays enthusiasm for her occupation

Spectacular foliage is on full display on this island nation

Overloaded trucks are a common sight within the city limits

day. I couldn't be more serious. As mentioned briefly in an earlier chapter, I felt very ill for five days during my stay here.

Now, for those of you who might be jumping to conclusions and speculating that the cat coffee I had consumed could be the most likely culprit leading up to my illness, I will say that I certainly do appreciate your enthusiasm. But you would be mistaken. It seems those dots simply don't add up, since I fell ill a few days prior to the consumption of that suspect coffee.

The most likely scenario which logically plays out in my mind is as such—a bite from a mosquito who was carrying and transmitted Dengue Fever. It seemed all the classic symptoms were at play.

A propane tank is attached to majority of these portable food stands

Motorbikes zip precariously through the streets of Bali

Watermelons are transported to a nearby market via a motorbike

Creature comforts are scarce and here, the bare necessities rule the day

I clearly remember the worst of the nights, as my fever climaxed, I had been huddling under the thick covers of my bed, while wearing a jacket and shivering like a leaf in a stiff autumn breeze. The inside temperature in my room was set at 74 Fahrenheit. I did wake up feeling somewhat better and remember feeling glad that I was still alive.

While traveling through Asia, you should not go home before seeing some rice fields, especially a terraced rice field. These unique fields, which are often carved in elegant rows into the sides of a mountain, are truly a spectacular sight to behold. Even if you lack a basic appreciation for agricultural practices, especially those who greatly differ from your home country,

Traveling on the bustling Balinese roads can be particularly harrowing for small children

Transporting lighter loads is obviously more typical for Americans

it is possible that you might take a moment to gaze out upon a neatly, seemingly obsessively manicured terrace, and find yourself surprised at how uniquely satisfying the scenery can be.

Farming a crop of rice has never been an easy task, especially when the work is done on such a treacherous mountainside, however; if you have an opportunity to visit such an agricultural wonder, please do. While in Indonesia, we did, and we harbor no regrets.

Typical rice terraces are sprinkled throughout the country

While Japan has an abundant number of impressively flat rice paddies, several Asian countries, including Indonesia and the Philippines, feature some strikingly captivating sheer terraces where rice flourishes.

Since I am not a rice farmer, I cannot tell you if farming the crop

on a flat surface is considerably optimal compared to that of a terrace. The way I understood it when explained to me is that when rice is farmed on a terrace, erosion and surface runoff are both significantly discouraged. This would seem indicative that a terraced property might be desirable

Rice terraces grace the rural areas surrounding Bali

to a completely flat area.

While we were enjoying our tour of several working rice farms here, we learned quite a bit about the crop. Throughout the world, nearly 100 million people are currently dependent on the production of rice. Approximately two-thirds of the world's total upland rice area is found in regions throughout Asia. Countries such as Thailand, Vietnam, Cambodia, Indonesia, China, and India are considered the most important producers of the

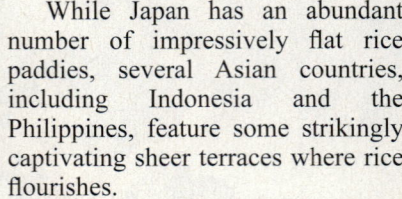

Workers toil in a rice field along the outskirts of Bali

A bicyclist refreshes with a light dinner
purchased at a food stall

A rice worker tends to the crop
after taking a midday break

A master of balance, a cyclist deftly navigates a narrow road

crop. According to various agricultural organizations, China produces and consumes the most rice than any other country in the world.

The crop requires intense irrigation, especially when planted in dry regions. Farmers typically irrigate heavily, and in some cases flood the fields with water. In Japan, for example, snowmelt can be utilized from the mountains during the spring. The water from the melted snow is collected in large reservoirs, where it is then applied to the fields at the time of planting or shortly thereafter. The crop is generally planted in mud or water, according to the farmer we spoke with.

After the crop has matured, irrigation typically ceases, and the soil is permitted to dry. Depending on the crop growth and the weather, the crop is usually harvested during a region's dry season, allowing for a highly coveted harvesting experience which also provides improved yields.

In considerably poorer regions of the world, such as Cambodia, farmers might only have enough land to provide for their

Upon resting for a brief moment, an elderly rice farmer continued his daily work in the fields

immediate family. These small parcels of land are typically used for production of rice crops, which will feed the hungry mouths of the poor farmer's children.

Rice is ubiquitous throughout Asia, of that there is no question. I probably never consumed as much rice in my entire previous years than I did during those fleeting four weeks of traveling throughout the region. During my stay, I guess you could say that I developed an acquired taste for the food staple; I needed to—or risk going hungry.

Smiling widely, a rice farmer labors under the intense rays of the summer sun

Indonesia also produces various other vegetative crops, including bananas, durian, rambutan, jackfruit, as well as tomatoes and sweet corn. There are scores of fruit and vegetable markets along the winding roadsides of Indonesia. It was here in Southeast Asia that I observed a distinct similarity between the work ethic of the Asian folks and that of the Amish and Mennonites living in prosperous Lancaster County.

Banana trees are not an unusual sight in Bali

Here, it seemed, every person who

Sheer drops in terrain provide a stunning backdrop at a rice farm

Banana, coconut, pineapple, and various other trees are spread prolifically along the rural roadsides

resided within Indonesia, had set up a roadside market, peddling their homegrown fruits and vegetables in similar fashion as the Anabaptists in North America. The only noticeable difference was, that these roadside stands were considerably more makeshift and strikingly impermanent compared to the typically fancy roadside stand that can be found along the side roads throughout Lancaster County.

It was at a remarkably poor-looking roadside market where I beckoned our driver to stop. By this time, we were deep in the countryside. Banana and pineapple trees were growing prolifically in the area, and their thick, heavy leaves were swaying slightly in the gentle sultry breezes. Up the road just a few meters, a young man was pushing a wheelbarrow laden with an overflowing amount of jackfruit. The contents of his wheelbarrow were nearly spilling, and the tires appeared

A typical fruit and vegetable market in Indonesia consists of items such as shown here

to be uncomfortably low in pressure.

I must have been lost in thought, too busy observing my surroundings, because our driver announced kindly, "We are here now."

Jeffery and I got out of our car and proceeded to walk toward the friendly lady who was managing her mobile fruit market, which she pulled behind her Kubota tractor. Smiling widely, she eagerly walked toward us, not waiting till we had approached her

Bananas and jack fruit are readily available at markets

market. She came bearing gifts, her hands were burdened with various fruits. She implored us to try a few free samples of her fresh fruits, breaking the skin of the fruits and shoving the ready to eat product into our hands.

She couldn't speak English very well, but here she was, wearing a bandana over her head to shield her from the summer sun, and a long dress, which featured small flowers on the print. She looked, by all accounts, like a dark-skinned Mennonite farmer lady from back home. And here was a woman, as poor as could be, breaking pieces of fruit for us wealthy American boys from the crop which she had grown. It reminded me of a passage in the Bible. ......*verily I say unto you, That this poor widow hath cast more in, than all they which have cast into the treasury: Mark 12:43 (KJV).*

Because of her generosity and kindness, Jeffrey and I walked away from her small roadside market after purchasing more fruit than we could eat within the following two days.

Far from the shores of the US, a choppy Indian Ocean beckons a tourist for a swim

CHAPTER 5
KIWI ADVENTURES AND AUSTRALIAN ANXIETY

Needing no introduction, the Sydney Opera House is viewed from a nearby park

The short flight was over before I had gotten an adequate amount of shut-eye. But here we were, gliding down onto the ever-elusive continent of Australia. Since I was a grade scholar, I had become infatuated with the continent and its very specific species of animals. Who doesn't consider kangaroos and koalas and the occasional platypus to be completely endearing?

Echidna can be spotted within the southern regions of the continent

With wonderful preconceived notions in my head, a broad smile broke my face as our plane touched down on the Australian tarmac. This was it, another one of my dreams had finally come true.

The immigration process here went quite well, even though we were told we must declare any souvenirs made from wood products, as well as any second pair of shoes we might have stashed in our luggage. I had a second pair along, and yes, they were immediately suspect.

"I see that you declared a pair of shoes," the smiling, genial customs official stated. "Are they wet? Do they contain any soil? Have you been hiking around on any contaminated farms or freshwater areas?"

Thankfully, I could answer each question with a negative. Most other countries did not require adherence to such strict guidelines to gain access into their country. New Zealand and Australia both required us to declare any wooden trinkets, shoes, and various other goods. Absolutely no bottled water was permitted to be taken aboard any New Zealand or Australian flights when entering those countries. Not even a sealed bottle of water. Flight attendants did, however,

Unique creatures are prevalent within Australia

ensure that each passenger received adequate beverages (from the aircraft's inventory) for personal consumption during the flights.

Sometimes our dreams and ideas can seem more flattering before they become reality. Has that ever happened to you? Apparently, my presuppositions of Australia had been painfully inaccurate.

Well, we made the best of it, but in this specific situation, Australia did not live up to the hype which I had created within my head. Well, not mainland Australia, anyway. The same cannot be said about the visually arresting island of

A small kangaroo pauses briefly before demonstrating its agility

Stunning red flowers take center stage as blue skies compete for equal attention

Botanical beauties abound within Australia

Tasmania. But we will get there in a bit. First, let's explore mainland Australia and the picturesque New Zealand Alps. We will be taking several train rides, so be sure to schedule your tickets in advance if you wish to join us, as the trains can easily sell out of all available accommodations.

To be fair, it certainly was quite memorable to stand in front of the Sydney Opera House, perhaps the most famous building in all of Australia. But that excitement wore off in a little while, and Jeffrey and I began developing a strong desire to see the Australian Outback. Prior to our leaving the states, little did we know exactly how vast the country of Australia really is. In order to see the Nullarbor Plains—the Outback and all its reddish soil—we would be required to purchase tickets for a seven-day train ride—for the price of several thousand US dollars.

After a few serious discussions between the two of us, we decided that before we would set aside such a sheer amount of money for a train ride, we would contemplate the situation as well as consider the logistical and financial implications such a decision might have on our itinerary.

The following morning, after having scored a few good hours of much needed sleep from yet another sizable time change, we had reached a decision before all the eggs and bacon from our hearty breakfast had been consumed. We decided against going. That is a serious chunk of money for any seven-day train ride. Bear in mind that we would have been gazing, perhaps with immeasurable disappointment, at a primarily treeless plain (Nullarbor in Latin means *no trees)* which covers a distance greater than seventy-thousand-square miles. Maybe that is a train ride you can take for me some time, I would enjoy hearing about your experience.

A few shorter train rides across the Australian countryside to connecting cities lost its luster rather quickly, and we decided to imitate the movements of the kangaroos which we saw and hop to our next destination—New Zealand. I personally

A few cathedrals and churches were scattered through Sydney

Deeply rooted trees offered an occasion to reflect upon the wonder of life itself

Unusual tree trunks provide an intriguing glimpse into the mysterious world of Australian botany

couldn't wait to get there, and besides, the folks in the Australian cities were way too much like Americans— rude, obnoxious, and remarkably inhospitable. Nothing at all like the exceptional Asian hospitality which we had grown so accustomed to for the past two weeks now. My heart ached to return to Asia, where the people wore million-dollar smiles on their dirt-streaked faces and seemed to have found the key to perpetual happiness. It simply had felt like we had developed a deep friendship with people of the Asian culture, and we wanted to quickly visit New Zealand and then head back to Asia.

Bidding farewell to the few kangaroos and koalas that we saw, we jumped in a taxi and headed for the airport. A mere two-and-a-half hours later found us passing through yet another customs gate before we were granted entry into the considerably friendlier country of New Zealand. (Here, the people seemed much more relaxed and polite).

The air was crisp and cool, and the sun shone brilliantly for the duration of our three-day visit. Autumn was well under-way here—in February—and I was delighted to be fortunate enough to experience a New Zealand autumn, since it is my favorite season of the year.

The Alps of New Zealand were certainly on our list of Kiwi adventures, and we purchased our train tickets early one chilly morning. A diesel-powered train treks deep into the mountains each day, and passengers on these comfortable rail expeditions better be prepared to see some breathtaking scenery.

A cloak of white mist blankets the lower tier of the mountainside

An open-air car was available for non-restricted viewing of the unique New Zealand scenery. Our train whistled past thousands of acres of premium farmland, as well as an enormous amount of forested areas. A few lakes, not to be outdone, also vied for our attention as I breathed in the freshest air that I have experienced since my exhilarating train ride through the Alps in

Switzerland in early winter of 2018.

In a way, I kind of wished the Alps here in New Zealand would be blanketed in layers of fresh snow. It was pleasant and enjoyable however, to visit in a season other than winter, since this provided us with perfect snapshots of iconic New Zealand farm life. The rolling meadows were still semi-green with life, but the fields were beginning to surrender to the prevailing

Arid regions persist during a typical autumn here

autumn elements, turning a beautiful shade of brown in their death.

Winter was coming to reclaim the landscape, and this couldn't have been more evident anywhere else than on the stiff chill which was borne on the persistent breezes. The summer had been a hot one, and lengthy, according to the locals. "I will be ready for winter and for colder weather," a local shared as we exclaimed how perfect the weather was here. And then he

Cattle graze in a sun-dappled New Zealand meadow

Soaring high above the mountains, a bird takes flight

quickly added, "It was a hot summer. You guys came at the right time. Now it is really nice."

Not only does the country have amazing weather, it also has a high concentration of sheep. In fact, there is such a dense population of sheep here that they outnumber humans. New Zealand is also quite well known for several excellent breeds of cattle as well as canines. The rich, fertile country is comprised of two islands, which are typically referred to as the north and the south islands. We only visited the southern island where the Alps are located, which had been our primary objective for a visit to this country.

The morning meal is of measurable importance within New Zealand

For the past year or so, a few farmers on the North Island, specifically in Wellington, have been milking herds of domesticated red deer. According to recent reports which followed the trend, the milk of red deer contains a delicate taste as well as a smoother texture and superior consistency when compared to the milk extracted from dairy cows. In 2018, the New Zealand farmers were using the red deer milk to create premium yogurt, cheese, and butter products.

During 2011, a severe earthquake hit the city of Christchurch, claiming the lives of more than a hundred people and injuring in excess of two thousand. The devastating effects wreaked havoc on the city's most recognized cathedral, structurally splitting it nearly in half. Eight years later, the church has not been rebuilt due to a squabble between the church officials and the government, according to information which the locals shared with us. I found it difficult to believe that a prominent church, the very landmark of the city, would not even receive proper care or at least be introduced to a rudimentary rebuilding program, so I took a short bus ride through the city streets to investigate on my own.

Sure enough, what I discovered was what the locals had told me that I would find. A beautiful church broken down the middle by a natural disaster. It just stood there, as if waiting for someone to begin its restructuring. Majority of the other buildings which had been devastated or destroyed within the immediate area had since been rebuilt or restored. But not the church. It sat in a semi-crumbled heap within the center of glittering new buildings.

My thoughts went to a more serious topic. Church splits which unfortunately take place from time to time throughout our Anabaptist communities can be nearly identical to this storied cathedral. Do we as Anabaptists make sure that our homes and properties are also shiny and glittering, while in our hearts, words, and minds we as Christians squabble in various manners with our brothers and sisters, ensuring that the Church cannot be rebuilt? The thought was uncomfortable, because I feared there could possibly be too much truth to that. My hope is such that my musings would be unfounded.

The squabble revolving around this iconic New Zealand cathedral may be resolved soon, the locals explained, but for now, various vendors have set up shop, selling their souvenirs and various other wares to tourists who continually flock here to catch a glimpse of a cathedral in ruins.

It may be of mild interest to note that the city received its name during the mid-1800s and is rumored to be named in honor of a cathedral in England. Today, Christchurch is the largest, most populous city on the South Island of New Zealand.

We could not stay and bask in the superbly sunny climate for the remainder of our scheduled

A train awaits as passengers disembark

journey, so we took it upon ourselves to pay the Anabaptists in Australia's Detention River Community a visit. Successful contact with them (via phone) was eventually achieved after a few failed attempts. After several previously unsuccessful phone calls, it had seemed as if we would be required to erase that stop from our already swelling itinerary.

Following our very warm, verbal welcome to the community after having talked on the phone with one of the elders of the conservative Anabaptists, Jeffrey and I booked a flight to Tasmania where we would meet them. On the way there, we experienced severe turbulence, in much the same way as we had when we flew to New Zealand. It seemed to take place at the same area, but it is difficult to ascertain land distance when one is 30,000 feet up in the clouds. However, the alarming turbulence occurred each time while we were flying over the Tasman Sea.

Our arrival at the tiny airport in Devonport, Tasmania was something to remember. It was a rather chilly night, with a prevailing breeze present. Our small 'hopper' plane touched down shortly before 9 PM. The airport's location was approximately an hour's drive from the Christian community in Detention River.

Daniel Russell, a member of the community, had driven to the airport and was waiting for us when we arrived. We had been told that this small airport lacked rental cars, and taxis were only available for us if we specifically notified our flight attendant at the

Curious yet guarded, a member of the kangaroo family chooses to appear uninterested in peering into the protruding lens of the camera

Nestled deep within the mountains, a sawmill stands idle

time which we boarded our plane. So, you can imagine how grateful we were to see Daniel's smiling face waiting to welcome us to the island.

Nearly buried from sight, a small farmhouse is situated at the foothills of a mountain range

Desolate, haunting scenes flourised within New Zealand's mountainsides

A road which seems to go nowhere wraps around the mountain deep in the wilderness

CHAPTER 6
AUSTRALIAN ANABAPTISTS AND JAPANESE BULLET TRAINS

A brilliant morning sun announces its arrival high above Tokyo, Japan

As our small car weaved through the darkness along the winding roads through the Tasmanian countryside, the threat of hitting a wandering wallaby was very real. For the duration of our nearly sixty-minute ride, Jeffery and I took great delight in conversing with our

Signage placed strategically at the entrance of the now-renamed Detention River Christian Community in Tasmania

driver Daniel and becoming more acquainted with the interesting lifestyle of the Anabaptist community which he was a part of.

"Welcome to Tasmania," Daniel had greeted us with a smile and a handshake just a few moments earlier. I must say, after having spent the previous several weeks traversing the world and seeing no other Anabaptist folks, it was rewarding and exciting to meet and talk with another person whom we shared similar values with.

The ride concluded too soon, as the three of us engaged in lively chatter,

resting briefly between the question and answer session which took place. I felt somewhat badly for Daniel, since Jeffrey and I must have peppered him with no less than two-hundred questions. But to be fair, one doesn't travel to the other side of the world to meet someone without diligently inquiring about the lifestyles

A bank of residences are flanked by gum trees and various botanical beauties at Detention River Christian Community

within the host's country.

We arrived at the community shortly before 10 PM and were greeted warmly once more by Daniel's parents. (No, we didn't hit any wallaby on our way there).

The following morning, after resting quite well in a guest house within the community, we enjoyed a home-cooked breakfast at Daniel's house. Daniel is married and is a young father. He has lived here in Tasmania with his wife and small family for several years now, but he was born in Canada.

Small buildings offer refuge for the community's free-range chickens

If memory serves me correctly, the small community here had been established around 1995 through a collaborative effort of Anabaptist men from the United States. Peter Hoover, a historian and author, was quite instrumental in establishing the community here in Detention River,

Dusk pushes onward as it envelops the serene Detention River community in late February, 2019

Tasmania. David Waldner and several other men from the Elmendorf Christian Community in Minnesota also played an integral part in relocating Anabaptist folks from the United States and Canada to Australia.

Today, the number of Anabaptist families who reside here on the communal property has diminished a bit in size. At the present time, the community is comprised of five families. In its nascence, nearly twice that many families had called Detention River Community their home. After living there for a few years, several families had opted to move back to the States.

Trevor Russell, Daniel's father, was very open and genuine as he and I discussed various aspects of the Christian and Anabaptist communities here in Tasmania as well as in the ones in North America. Throughout our conversation, Trevor explained that he would be excited and thrilled to be able to connect with American Anabaptist folks, primarily to market the various unique wood products which the community produces.

"We would be interested in marketing our wood products to the Anabaptist people in America," Trevor explained. "Here on the island, we have several species of wood that are specifically unique to our region. The wood which we use to create various pieces of furniture are very specific; these types of wood simply do not exist natively anywhere else." (Huon pine and deciduous beech are among the woods which are specific to the island state).

A sizable woodworking shop is located on their sprawling property, and the men labor within the walls of the building whenever they can. This type of work is not their only source of income, however, and true to form—like most other Anabaptists—they busy themselves with other work

Stacks of firewood, arranged in a neat and organized manner, located at the edge of the community's meadows

as well. A metal shop is also located at the far end of the property, where a few of the men and boys spend most of their time throughout the day, primarily producing hay troughs which will be used on dairy or cattle farms. These round feeding troughs are generally placed in meadows or barns.

A few cows provide the community with fresh milk, and they enjoy grazing on the spacious meadows located on the community grounds behind a neat row of plain-looking houses. The residences are clean and modest but lack unnecessary outward (or interior) adornment. Towering peppermint gum trees wrap around the meadows and nearby orchard.

Growing a modest crop of vegetables and fruit doesn't happen on its own. Well, perhaps the growing part does, but certainly many hands are required to care for the crops. We walked through the orchard on a cool morning, the grass still wet from the early morning dew. Neat rows of peach trees and apples trees lined the orchard.

Round bales of hay provide many nutritious meals for cattle at a neighboring meadow near the Detention River

Some of the fruits and vegetables are eaten fresh, while the remainder is frozen or canned for consumption at a later time.

The community's cow gazes into the distance and seems unfazed and unimpressed by the intruding lens of the camera

Many times, throughout our short visit, I was surprised at how nearly identical these Australian Anabaptists live to those of us who reside within the borders of North America. Some distinct differences are present, while stark similarities prevail.

The community garden is within proximity of a small paved road, which features a relaxed amount of traffic. Here within this part of the island, it seems as if everyone knows each other. In fact, when Daniel takes us on a tour of the island the following day, he waves hello to the drivers of most vehicles, verbally acknowledging to Jeffery and myself, that he knows the occupants of the passing cars.

Just a few short miles down the road from the community, waits a picturesque, remote national park, bedecked with various scenic jewels. The park, which is referred to as Rocky Cape National Park, is rewardingly rugged and wild, in much the same manner as you might expect a portion of land, untouched by humans, to be.

It was here, while walking along the pristine sandy beaches of Rocky Cape Park, that I was the farthest from home as I had ever been in my life. Approximately 10,226 miles, give or take a few. In a way, it really kind of felt incredibly far, too. Because right before my very eyes was a

Colorful crests such as these provoke an ethereal ambiance at Rocky Cape National Park

visually beautiful feast which I could never have imagined—unlike anything I have ever seen in the United States or Europe. Large, multi-colored cragged cliffs rose prominently and proudly, jutting their way deep into the sky. Below, the wild waters of the Bass Strait crashed with fervor against the worn, fatigued rocks.

Somewhat surprisingly, there is a significant portion of verdant farmland located on the island. Throughout the day, we passed several large dairy and sheep farming operations. The animals were typically grazing contentedly in lush pastures, with

Restless waters lap eagerly at the rocks along the Bass Strait in Tasmania

Prominent, memorable rock formations rise into the skies at the edge of Bass Strait

the occasional looming mountain serving as a magnificent backdrop. When viewed from the sky, the island resembles a heart-shape, with both its maximum length and width spanning some odd two-hundred-miles. The island is slightly larger than Sri Lanka, which is an island located in the Indian Ocean. Australia has many expansive states, of which Tasmania is the smallest. Twenty-six-thousand-plus acres comprise the island, and you will find several airports and modestly sized cities throughout the island.

On the afternoon of the last day that we spent within the community, Daniel drove us to a lookout point located approximately twenty minutes from his residence. We hiked up the lookout and walked around the top. Many species of trees were growing on the top of the expansive cliff. Although the

Speckled with vibrant, multi-colored cliffs which extend far into the sparkling waters, Rocky Cape National Park is a must-see for many tourists who venture near the Edge of the World

wind swept cruelly across some areas of the steep bluff, there were other areas which offered refuge from the prevailing winds. For several minutes, we indulged in amazing panoramic

High atop the grassy hills of the pastoral island of Tasmania, cattle graze contentedly

views, completely in awe of what God had created.

In the scientific community, the steep, rocky area which we had been standing on top of is referred to as an ancient volcanic plug. The scenic attraction is located on the edge of the historic village of Stanley. *Welcome to the Edge of the World,* a sign situated at the town's entry point, greets visitors from all over the world.

A winding path leads to a most enchanting scene along the outlying areas at picturesque Rocky Cape National Park

The lookout is understandably the main attraction for visitors who dare to brave the journey to this remote area in northwest Tasmania. *The Nut*, as it is called, largely due to its shape, spirals nearly 470-feet in height and features a flat top, which allows for lengthy walks spanning more than a mile. While traversing across its vast top, we saw numerous wallaby (in similarity to tiny kangaroos), many

The Nut, a majestic natural wonder, paints a commanding pose against the dreary horizon in Tasmania

unique species of birds, and a host of other wildlife. But thankfully, no snakes.

Historically, the town of Stanley is steeped in royalty, and at one point in time, served as an important trading post for various merchant ships. The tiny town also utilized the rays of a lighthouse many years ago. The charming coastal village also hosted a major motion picture production several years ago.

Possibly another point of interest is that several of the prominent signs which are displayed on a historic hotel building here were

designed by members of a Bruderhof Community located on the mainland of Australia. For those of you who might be unfamiliar with the Bruderhof lifestyle, suffice it to say that members of these communities belong to a branch of the Anabaptist family tree and live communally in a similar fashion as the Hutterites do.

Shortly after we had arrived back at the community from our little jaunt around the edge of the sheer bluff, seemingly atop the world, we hungry men, without further delay, made our way to the communal kitchen where a

Whispy cloud cover blankets the sandy beaches of Rocky Cape, Tasmania

most tantalizing scent was carried on the breeze from an open window. Mealtimes here within the community are relaxed and genial, except of course on Quiet Night. During those nights, discussions are kept to an absolute minimum. In fact, sometimes no words might be exchanged at all—until after dinner, of course, when everyone has moved away from the table.

Trevor explained that the community has come to value Quiet Night, which permits them a few moments to consume their evening meal while they meditate and reflect upon matters of the spirit. Quiet Night was scheduled to take place on the evening which Jeffrey and I were visiting, however, the solemn dinner was cancelled at the last minute. "Since we have guests, we will reschedule Quiet Night for another time," Trevor announced before we each took our seats at the table.

Various tables lined the middle of the spacious dining hall, and during the several meals in which we participated, cafeteria style was the order of the day. Grace is verbally acknowledged prior to the meal, and most times, immediately following the meal, while everyone is yet seated, a song is sung from a large song sheet which is temporarily taped to the wall of the dining hall. Upon the conclusion of the hearty, homecooked

Overlooking the rippling waters of Bass Strait, tourists and locals alike can indulge in the natural beauty atop one of the many cliffs at Rocky Cape

meal, everyone assists in the washing and drying of dishes. Yes, even the menfolk help. I understand they assist with dishes after every meal.

The family structure is revered here within the Anabaptist community, and most evenings are spent gathering at one of the community member's homes to enjoy extended fellowship as the last streaks of light leave the Australian skies.

Speaking of skies, it is soon time for Jeffrey and me to soar up beyond the clouds again. Daniel, in his generosity and kindness, has agreed to drive us to the nearby airport so that we might catch our plane to Japan. Tokyo, the world's largest city, is now within the crosshairs of our travel scope.

We have purchased a seven-day Japan rail pass and have an appointment with a bullet train. Little did we know, at the time, that we were about to travel at speeds of 190 mph—on the ground.

Our flight would have several stopovers, so early the next morning, Jeffrey and I boarded a plane from Tasmania to Melbourne and weren't even

Unique trees and vegetation thrive atop The Nut, which pierces more than 400 feet into the Tasmanian skies near the town of Stanley

Breathtaking hues hint to the promises of another blessed day

Delicate and elegant, various pastries pose artfully behind glass along the expansive corridors at Narita International

Barely decipherable to the American eye, a receipt from the Toyko Pizza Hut indicates a delicious bargain was snagged

required to pass through metal detectors or any sort of luggage or body scanners. Granted, it was a small hopper plane capable of transporting no more than 80 people, but still, we found it nearly unfathomable that no security checks would take place prior to boarding.

For example, even though we lacked security scans in Tasmania, at least the airport security officer in Melbourne had the courtesy of engaging Jeffrey in dialogue the moment we placed our luggage on the scales. "Carrying any explosives today, Mate?"

The historic port of Stanley, Tasmania

As we fastened our seatbelts, and with the flight attendant urgently explaining the safety features of the aircraft, our heads were still swirling with precious memories which had been formed throughout our two-day visit to the wonderful community in Detention River.

Far from Lancaster, Pennsylvania, serene beach scenes dominate the landscape at Rocky Cape National Park, Tasmania

Various trees, some remarkably tall, stood proudly atop the wind-beaten crests of The Nut in Tasmania

Tufts of vegetation persists atop a jagged cliff overlooking the Bass Strait in Tasmania

CHAPTER 7
MAJESTIC MOUNTAINS AND EXCEPTIONAL JAPANESE HOSPITALITY

Stately and majestic, Mount Fuji thrills the hearts of tourists from near and far

Japan has a lot to offer in terms of rich history, cultural diversity, and eye-popping scenery. After spending a few hours within the country's border, I was already beginning to miss everything about Japan—and I hadn't left yet.

The coolness of the floating mist persuasively envelops everything in its proximity

We had a full itinerary here, since Jeffery and I both wished to see the cities of Hiroshima and Nagasaki. Mount Fuji was also on the hit-list.

Also, I simply can't leave Japan before witnessing the throngs of humanity at the famed Shibuya Crossing, the busiest pedestrian crossing in the world. Several times each workday, at the height of foot traffic, more than three-thousand humans cross the street in multiple directions every four minutes—or so they say. We were going to be amongst that wonderful maize of humanity in just a few hours. Well, to be sure, the throngs of people were more like a dense jungle than a maize.

First things first, though. Let's validate our seven-day rail pass and become acquainted with the best train system in the world, Japan's very own *Shinkansen* (a railroad system carrying high-speed passenger trains).

You may be surprised to learn that the initial idea of a premium high-speed rail system here in Japan very nearly didn't reach fruition. Just like when an imaginative person has many new, odd ideas, many more people will be waiting in line to take a cheap jab at the unorthodox idea. Back in the 1950s, when two Japanese businessmen introduced the idea of an extensive, high-speed rail network which they surmised could weave across the country, connecting passengers to various cities, the ambitious ideas of the two men were reportedly met with utter disdain. A

Bequiling checkered prints adorn the floor of a slow commuter train operating outside Toyko's main hub

Majority of pedestrians from all corners of the globe converge upon the famed crossing, weilding cellphones which facilitate the ease of snapping satisfying selfies

Awaiting its departure signal, a bullet train relaxes at a station for a brief moment before transporting passengers to their desired destinations

few people even went as far as calling the idea preposterous and labeling the two visionaries as "mad" and "fools" on the front pages of the national newspapers.

But thankfully, these two men didn't allow the weaker minds of their feeble countrymen to dissuade them from their noble purpose of introducing what is today known as 'bullet trains.' The Shinkansen system is truly an impressive

Exemplifying aggressive curves and boundless agility, a Japanese bullet train arrives at a station

technological marvel for which millions of humans are grateful for. Since its birth more than fifty years ago, the Shinkansen of Japan has transported more than 10 billion passengers. That's more than the number of humans which are said to currently occupy the planet.

From all these mind-bending speeds of which the trains travel at each day, it is certainly notable that their safety record is impressive—perfect, even. Some trains on the Shinkansen system travel at speeds in excess of two-hundred-miles-per-hour. Not all the trains possess the capability of reaching such fear-inducing speeds, but some do. The average speed of majority of the trains within this system can and do travel at an average of 190-mph. To put this into perspective, when

A string of city lights begin to twinkle along a narrow Nagasaki street as dusk becomes evident

As night falls, the city of Nagasaki comes to life, its lights emitting a pleasant and welcoming glow

you glance out the window of these racing trains, everything outside is largely indistinguishable and passes by in a blur.

Also, if you are a passenger on a train which has stopped to off-load passengers at a station, and another train traveling right beside yours on a nearby track just mere inches away passes by, you can feel the body of your train 'inhaling' and then 'exhaling' upon the completed passing of the other train. For example, the opposing train is moving so fast (190 mph or so) just inches from your train, that it seems like a significant likelihood that your train, which is in a current state of inertia, to be swallowed whole by the vacuum the other train creates when it races by in a screaming blur.

Such an exhilarating experience certainly isn't for the weak at heart. But it is, however, quite appealing to those of us who enjoy getting from point A to point B in as little time as humanly possible. Fair warning— on the bullet trains, you simply can't stop and smell the flowers—you will need to book a ticket with Amtrak if you wish to do that.

You might have heard it said that riding the rails has become one of my favorite pastimes. Such a statement would largely be correct, especially if those rails are located within Europe or in highly developed regions throughout Asia.

I have, however, on several occasions, thoroughly enjoyed coast-to-coast journeys throughout the United States via our domestic passenger rail carrier. But the fleeting enjoyment from that experience was eclipsed and eventually

A heater, whose very appearance whispers of days gone by, casts a gentle warmth inside a restaurant in Fujinomiya

Architecture which evokes palatial pomp is seen from Hiroshima's Old City district

permanently erased after I received a healthy taste of what high-speed rail travel really is like. I wonder, if we became accustomed to trains here which would be capable of traveling at 200 mph, would we be satisfied? Or would that excitement wane, leaving our baser urges sadly unsatisfied? We might then only harbor a desire to go faster yet—maybe 300 mph?

Throughout the Shinkansen's storied history, there have been zero passenger fatalities as of April 2019. This is certainly notable, because there are dozens of these bullet

The author pauses briefly at Tokyo's Narita International Airport

trains whipping along at breakneck speeds on various rail lines in the most earthquake-prone country on the planet. The infrastructure of this impressive rail system is truly remarkable—I wish each of you could have seen it.

While here, Jeffrey and I kept close tabs on exactly how punctual the Japanese rail system is. I must say, we were disappointed. We had been hoping that we would be one of the very precious few people who can say that we were passengers on a bullet train that departed or arrived at the station late—even if it was just by thirty seconds. But for the three days which we occupied the bullet trains, we never arrived or departed late, it was always perfectly and obsessively

punctual. In fact, there has been one time, several years ago, that a train operator on the Shinkansen system had departed the station less than thirty seconds off-schedule. This was utter madness. The seemingly minor infraction resulted in the train system publicly apologizing in the national newspaper. Imagine that for a moment.

But punctuality isn't the only virtue that is highly revered in Japanese culture. Cleanliness is too. Everything from restaurants to train stations to sidewalks were kept impossibly clean here. Would you believe me if I told you that

Pale blue skies blanket the horizon as several tourists enter the gracefully designed building

train station attendants spend countless hours polishing the handrails and doorknobs located within the stations? Well, I saw them do just that, on several occasions. How about a creepy wheeled robot who goes about Tokyo's busiest airport, dutifully cleaning low, easy to reach glass windows and various other objects? They have that here, too. What about toilets that are outfitted with more cycles to deposit water with than your shower does? Check. The cleanest streets of any major city which I have visited so far? Also, check.

All this appealed quite strongly to my slight obsession with personal hygiene. Living here would be fun, I thought, but also quite exhausting. How clean would be considered *clean enough?* This American was about to be in for a complete cultural shock the moment he crossed into Lao territory in a few short days—we will dive into that later, let's first indulge in some iconic sights associated with Japan.

Rice paddies can be seen in abundance from the train windows near Nagasaki

Throughout our four-day visit to the island nation, we saw many ancient castles and temples, some which dated back to the twelfth century. The sheer speeds of the bullet trains made it possible for us to extensively travel across the greater part of Japan, all within a few short days. The country is quite lengthy and slender, and our destination cities of Hiroshima and Nagasaki, are spread far apart. Not to worry though, we always got to our destinations on time. With the help of the Shinkansen, we successfully traveled through various prefectures, covering more

道しるべ

すべての人には
その個性の美しさがある

ご自由にお取り下さい

広島市遺族会
安古市支部

Worshippers frequent buildings such as this one located near Hiroshima,
adhering to a ritualistic form of physically expressive worship

儀式殿

Beautiful architecture graces the historical region located outside the main city hub of Hiroshima

The snowcaps of Mount Fuji peek from behind a blooming bush near a popular lookout area

than 1,600 miles in one day, all while staying on the rails.

During our travels we whipped past perfectly manicured rice paddies and hundreds of plastic greenhouses. It struck me as odd that here in Japan, my eyes would behold a significantly greater number (higher density) of greenhouses than what I typically see while traveling within the immediate areas of my home country. The plastic structures did look just a tad different than those which sprinkle the landscape of Lancaster County, however, there were also some striking similarities among them.

You might wonder if traveling on the bullet trains is a noisy, annoying experience. I would be quick to tell you that the affair is quite pleasant and unbelievably quiet. At times, travel within the fast-moving trains was uncomfortably quiet—it seemed as if it were only sensible that the trains would emit an audible decibel of sound.

Snow melt complements the rippling, flowing waters near Mount Fuji

Takeoff, yes, that is what I will call it, is very smooth as well. When leaving the stations, the train begins to creep slowly and then wastes no time in reaching smooth and persistently increased rates of speeds the moment the last car clears the station platforms. The conclusion of each journey is very smooth as well, considering that just mere moments before, the train had been traveling well-over one-hundred-miles-per-hour.

When the train reaches its final terminal (station), the train operator—shall we call him

Exquisite fruits are meticulously arranged at a market in Nagasaki

a pilot—steps out onto the station platform and bows deeply and respectfully to each of his passengers who walk past him on their way to the station egress points. This behavior is typical and not only reserved for the train operator.

The ticket attendants who passed through each car, scanning and checking tickets, also paused and bowed deeply to the occupants within the car, before making their way to the next train car. All this bowing seemed a bit excessive and unnecessary, especially when the passenger who had been sitting on the shared seat beside me got up to leave. The train had apparently arrived at his desired destination, and he began rummaging around in the overhead lockers for his belongings. Pausing briefly, the well-dressed businessman, moving with the finesse usually only practiced by surgeons or therapists, smiled and bowed politely to me before turning on his heels and disappearing into the lights of the brightly lit station.

So, for several days, as this behavior continued to escalate, Jeffrey and I contemplated the reality of returning to our fast-paced homeland, where instead of everyone bowing deeply to us, they would rather take pleasure in running over us in their haste to get to wherever they are going. Here in hospitable Japan, even the waiters in the restaurants paused and bowed to the patrons who were sitting in each

Looming proudly in the distance, Mount Fuji looks on as vehicles await at the taxi stand outside a popular tourist destination in Japan

It is uncommon to see Mount Fuji completely unshrouded, as cloud cover consistently gravitates around its peaks

A darkened alley in Nagasaki. Not all of Japan was immaculate.

Eager eyes peer from behind an eccentric market stall along the quiet side streets of Nagasaki

table as they passed by on their way to deliver trays of food. It was almost unbelievable—it seemed so dreadfully inefficient to us.

It might be needless to reiterate, that I was remarkably impressed with the exceptional hospitality which encompasses the Japanese culture, and I do wish to adapt and integrate a bit more of their politeness into my daily routine. I can be so hurried and rude at times, of this, I was painfully made aware of during my visit.

The public buses here were also unlike any buses I had previously occupied. They were immaculate. How do they keep things so clean? Also, why can't we have such nice things here in America?

Sparkling waters fall in the foreground as Japan's iconic mountain serves as a stunning backdrop

Water flows steadily from the jagged rocks at a tourist trap near Mount Fuji

Colorful hues are captured as the sun shines brightly on the mist which is
emitted from the waterfalls as it flows past a small cabin

Towering high above the throngs of rushing
humanity, a clock at Nagasaki terminal
displays the time

Water flows gently past elegant architecture near Hirsohima

Mount Fuji was spotted from the sparkling windows of our bus around mid-morning. It was a gorgeous day, and brilliant sunshine flooded the area surrounding the majestic snow-capped mountain. Reaching into the clouds at a height of 12,388-feet, the mountain intimidates and inspires all who gaze at its beauty. There was considerable cloud cover shrouding the peak on the day which Jeffrey and I visited, however; it was still an enjoyable time to walk in the shadows of the mighty Japanese mountain. It reminded me of a Bible verse in *Nahum 1:5: The mountains quake at him, and the hills melt, and the earth is burned at his presence…*

CHAPTER 8
CULTURED CITIES AND KOREAN CAPERS

Shibuya Crossing, where thousands of pedestrians cross every few minutes during rush hour

As indicated in the previous column, you and I have a bit of walking to do here in Japan before we jump a flight to Seoul, South Korea. Let's go for a casual stroll through Tokyo's Shibuya Crossing. Nothing strenuous or stressing—only the world's busiest pedestrian crossing. If you

stay close and follow me, I promise that I will get you through the mass of humanity without getting jostled too much.

I don't believe I have ever seen so many humans in one spot. Well, yes, I guess I did, when I was in New York City during a New Year's Eve event several years ago. But still, that seems to pale in comparison to the number of humans here in the largest city in the world, which is home to 28 million human beings —and counting— milling about the sprawling city center. It seemed

Morning and evening pedestrian traffic can be especially chaotic in Japan's busy railway stations

It appears as if numbers are nearly universal

as if my eyes could scarcely behold the busy sight.

Upon reaching the Crossing, we had to battle our way through a jungle of people just to get to the crosswalk. A light cycles every few minutes, permitting a mass exodus of people which fan from various train stations and subway tunnels, to safely cross the street.

Large, towering skyscrapers loom in every direction here, dwarfing the sea of people who anxiously await the signal, permitting them to cross. When the pedestrian light turns, indicating that it is ok to shuffle across the street, nearly three-thousand pedestrians and bicyclists hurry to their desired destinations.

It seems as if some of the pedestrians

Rush hour pedestrian traffic snarls the busiest railway stations in Shinagawa, Japan

may not have had a clear motive or plan for their travels. Case in point—two American boys from the farm—who relished in their new-found delight in crossing the human-deluged street several times. Once, they crossed the street out of necessity, and the remainder of the times, it

Slightly elevated rail systems are generally utilized a good distance from the stations

was just for fun. Even though I generally enjoy humans, I was, in time, adequately ready to leave the swarming city behind.

After we boys had gotten our fill of the famed Crossing, we concluded that the time had come to jump on a flight to South Korea. Several folks had told us throughout our journey that they would never visit the country. Too much unrest, they cited. And too close in

Mountains can be seen in the distance from many of Japan's railway stations

proximity to their volatile Northern neighbors. Oh well, I still couldn't manage to shake the curiosity from my soul. I just needed to see it and experience it for myself, I reasoned.

While in South Korea, a day trip via bus to the DMZ (the dematerialized zone) weighed on my mind quite heavily. Should we go? Would it be safe? The tour would get us as close to the North Korean border than I ever thought I wanted to be in my lifetime, I think. It sounded all so very exciting. We must go.

Onions, among various other vegetables, are seen from the sidewalk of a busy South Korean city

Fruits and vegetables are abundant within the heart of Seoul's business district

Chestnuts remain a staple at many street markets in South Korea, and are prolifically sold throughout the country

It is interesting what a good night's sleep can do to a person. After having slept well that night, I woke up feeling a bit uneasy about our trip to the DMZ. Would it be appropriate for us to go, as Christians? I wasn't sure. Nevertheless, I still really wanted to go; I was still wearing the cloak of curiosity.

So, I shared my thoughts—at length—with Jeffrey while we chugged coffee and consumed the last bits of bacon in the hotel's dining area.

Upon the conclusion of our hurried morning meal, we took a train to the city center, where we walked around a bit, observing the colorful markets. Everything was being sold here, from blankets to backpacks, to beautiful quilts (yes, they looked like Amish ladies may have produced them), to roasted sweet corn on a grill, as well as sushi. Lots of sushi. And live fish—they were swimming around in buckets which lined the streets. It was, quite literally, the largest outdoor market I had ever been to in my life.

Cheery and abundantly colorful items are sold at every corner of Seoul's expansive street markets

The market area was trashy, and we even saw several homeless people rummaging through trash cans for food. It was sad. But I guess that sight plays out daily in American cities too.

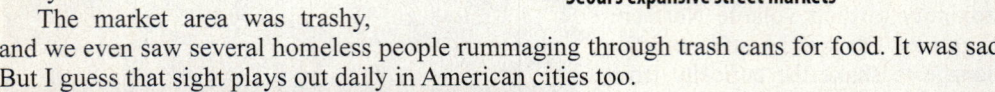

The handicapped man who pushed bravely through the busy streets of Seoul

I will also never forget this one crippled man; in particular. He had lost both his legs and most of his thighs. It was a chilly, damp day, and he was crawling along on the cold asphalt, pushing a small cart with his one hand as he weaved through the throngs of rushing passersby and street vendors. The pitiful sight chilled me. It was heartbreaking. Here was a poor man who was probably homeless, unloved, and uncared for, determinedly pushing his way through a mass of humanity in order to get somewhere. A small basket, complete with letters written in the Korean language, was placed atop his cart. I don't know what it said, since I can't decipher Korean, but in this small basket, a few coins jingled as he pushed the cart along, ever so slowly.

For some reason, whenever I reflect upon my journey to South Korea, I think of him. Even though I met dozens of other people there, I simply cannot erase that scene from my mind. Nor should I want to. That I could not offer him a decipherable word of encouragement or comfort will haunt me for a long time. The language barrier was insurmountable. Even though I still had all my limbs perfectly intact, I felt helpless. And guilty.

We continued to walk through the market for a few more hours, until our legs grew weary. It seemed as if the harried look on our faces may have spoken too loudly, been too obvious, perhaps. Because a lady who operated a small food stall approached us and implored us to sit and rest for a spell, and to indulge in her hot food. I was way too tired to argue against her well-thought-out plan, so I just went with it. I motioned to Jeffrey that I am going to grab a bite to eat. Taking a quick look at the establishment, he briefly countered his concerns.

But I didn't listen to him and followed the lady into the small diner. I immediately became aware of my mistake. I had again been a bit too rash in my decision making and a bit too lax in my discernment. The small diner smelled distinctly unpleasant and was packed with what

primarily appeared to be locals. On the wall in front of me, a menu printed only in Korean, greeted my eyes. It was too late to turn around and leave now—she had already seated us and had done so with a friendly yet all-too-satisfied smile.

That day, I ordered from a menu which I had no solid idea as to what I may receive. That

Spicy soups simmer atop a stove at an open street market in Seoul

might unnerve some of you, and I guess it would be less than honest if I said I hadn't been slightly uncomfortable myself, but the thrill of the unfamiliar can also be somewhat addictive and adrenaline-inducing as well.

Various vegetables and meats are cooked to diners' specifications at street markets in South Korea

Just a few days prior to this South Korean diner dilemma, I had stopped in at a 7-Eleven store in Japan and had boldly purchased a neatly packaged box of something which I had no idea of its contents. I shook the small box a little before I committed to the purchase, I had surmised that there were crackers inside. I so strongly wished for a salty treat. But I was sadly mistaken.

When I opened the box some time later while sitting in the comfy seat of the bullet train, I had realized that my salty treat would just be wishful thinking. Upon tearing open the box, the mystery contents had been revealed. Chocolate cake. I hate chocolate.

Moving ahead to the present, I was delighted to learn that I wouldn't be quite as disappointed with this lady's Korean diner. What she brought to me was edible, for sure, but also incredibly spicy. Spicy to the point where I began to cough, and my tongue remained numb for a few minutes after I put my spoon and fork down—rather loudly—out of despair at the pangs of pain which were ravaging my mouth.

Placing an order from a menu such as this one provides a barrage of challenges for the average American

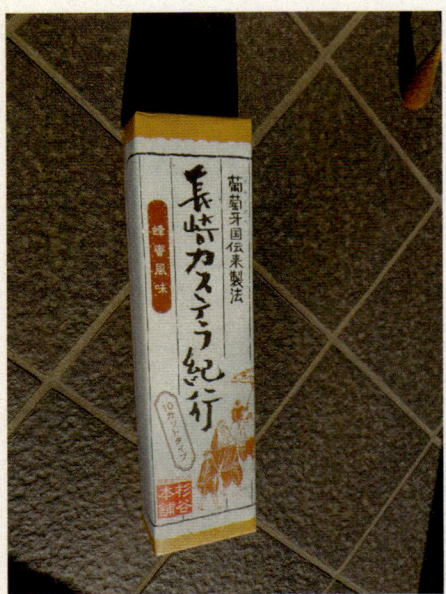

The box which disappointed so immensely.
A chocolate cake was lurking inside

Maybe Jeffrey had been right, I should have been more selective of our eating establishment.

Anyway, about the wonderful benefits of a good night's sleep as I mentioned a couple paragraphs ago. We eventually decided against going to the DMZ, mostly because we didn't feel comfortable being tossed in the middle of what we considered to be an escalating (albeit not new) situation between two countries.

Even though the city of Seoul was largely receptive to Americans, we were left with a distinctly uneasy feeling which pitted in the center of our stomachs. Military choppers were buzzing loudly in the skies above Seoul, which is located considerably close (mere miles) to the North Korean border.

Aware of the developing and maturing civil unrest in this immediate area of the globe, Jeffrey

The steps of a subway station are littered with items which
merchants are eager to sell

verbalized his discomfort more than once while we were occupying the streets which seemed to feature an over-abundance of heavily armed military personnel. Perhaps the steady stream of helicopters and bands of military officers which silently stood as solemn sentries at each major intersection of the city was nothing new. Maybe it was just another boring day for the residents of Seoul.

Suffice it to say that both Jeffrey and I were eager to leave the country. I think we exhaled sighs of relief when we arrived unscathed at Incheon International's departure terminals. I guess we are much more comfortable seeing robins soar in the skies than we are watching foreign military helicopters cutting up the clouds.

And with that, we will bid farewell to the Koreans and jump on over to Laos, a relatively poor, impoverished country in Southeast Asia. The country is petite and landlocked between Cambodia, Vietnam,

Signage which largely remains indecipherable to American eyes
covers nearly every available advertising spot in Seoul

Mere miles from the North Korean border, this seemingly serene place is typically on high alert for any threats regarding its exquisite architecture and established infrastructure

Myanmar, and Thailand.

The night air was heavy and stagnant as we passed through the immigration lines at the small international airport. We were in the process of completing our paperwork when an immigration official approached us and informed us that we don't need to complete the document. Glancing at our partially completed papers, he said, "It's ok. Just go. You may go now."

Not sure if it was a setup and that we wouldn't be subjected to an immigration fine at the counter when we presented our incomplete papers, we smiled and mentioned to him that we would like to quickly write down a few crucial details on the immigration forms. He seemed to understand and returned our smile. Walking away, he stood there in a corner and eyed us for a bit while we continued to write. This behavior of his seemed erratic, and Jeffrey and I became increasingly distrustful of him.

Approaching us again, he reiterated that we should pass through immigration now. Ok, this time we took the hint and placed our pens down on the counter. We desired avoiding a scene or any disturbance. We cleared immigration with our incomplete documents without a hitch. I guess the immigration fee ($35.USD) which we needed to pay to enter was really the most important element here.

That night, we hailed a taxi and watched in awe as the driver navigated through an ocean of buzzing motorbikes on the dusty, unpaved city alleyways towards our hotel. As soon as we arrived at our accommodations, we jumped out of the dust-covered car and attempted to pay our driver for services rendered. But he wouldn't take our American money, and neither would he accept our Laos currency. He flat out refused.

South Korea's Gyeongbokgung Palace provides a palatial peek at meticulous architecture

I extracted a credit card, thinking that he might wish to be paid via plastic. The battle wasn't going to be won that way either. He kept pointing to my wallet and muttering something which was indecipherable to us. Surely, he wasn't after the blank check I carried in my wallet, was he?

The situation escalated. He didn't want our cash, but it was clear that he wanted us to pay him for the ride. "Why won't you take our money?" I asked, frustrated.

He just shook his head and raised his voice even more, still pointing desperately at my wallet. It was ok up until the point where he handed me my money back and then reached for my wallet. I felt he crossed a line of professionalism there, and I began to become quite distressed.

A moat provides a reflective moment as tourists pause to catch their reflections as they visit the palace grounds

A legitimate coffee shop along a nearly abandoned alley in Seoul

A simple and elegant approach to dessert at a trendy restaurant in South Korea

Arid landscapes, seen from the small window of a speeding passenger train in South Korea

Bursting with sweetness, strawberries are prominently displayed at a street market in Seoul

Artificial intelligence scampers around South Korea's Incheon International Airport

Hundreds of vendors hawk the bustling streets of Seoul for hours each market day

Located at the edge of the city square, thousands of pedestrians rush past this structure each day

Prices ranging from 3000 to 20,000 Won are displayed by fruit merchants

Sweet corn sells for 2000 Won at a street market in Seoul

Pedestrians and cars clog the vibrant, bustling city center of Seoul

Personnel employed by the city of Hiroshima clean rubbish from its streets daily

Remains of a structure which survived the bombing of Hiroshima in 1945

Scenes such as this pass by at seemingly lightning speeds from the windows of a Japanese bullet train

Spotted just outside the busy city centers of Seoul, South Korea

Strangely enticing, a plate heaped high with green spaghetti is served at an upscale eatery outside Seoul's main district

The promise of a new day began by consuming several beverages, including a thick, yellow breakfast soup

The city streets can be seen from high atop a palace in Hiroshima, Japan

The owner of this bicycle appeals for an end to nuclear states

Uniquely shaped structures such as this one can be seen throughout Seoul. This is a photo of a hotel the author slept in.

Trees flank the sides of an artfully designed structure outside Seoul

CHAPTER 9
DODGING MOTORBIKES AND VISITING MONASTERIES IN LAOS

A common scene along the busy Laos streets

"What am I not understanding? What does this guy want from us?" I asked the concierge who had been standing outside our hotel and observing our situation. Tonight's choice of accommodations seemed to mimic that of a heavily fortified compound, with three guards at the entrance, one of them armed.

It was a sultry night, and bringing my handkerchief to my face, I quickly wiped the prevailing beads of sweat from my face as I awaited his reply. The persistent ripples of sweat poured partly due to the anxiety which kept building within me, and the remainder of the blame for the sweat fell squarely on the oppressive heat.

Exhausted from the day's travels, a rickshaw driver relaxes during a mid-afternoon break in Siem Reap

Jeffrey and I had found ourselves in a bit of a predicament here in the dimly lit, dusty side streets of Laos. Upon egressing our taxi car and attempting to pay the fare in either American or Lao currency, our efforts had been vigorously refuted by an increasingly irate driver.

"Let me see what the matter is," the concierge replied. "I will talk to your driver."

After conversing in elevated tones in the Lao language, the concierge smiled and approached us. "He says that you are trying to pay him with new American currency. He cannot accept. He needs the old currency, that was printed many years ago. The new picture on your bills, it's no good."

Well, that was a new one (no pun intended) for us. I tried to explain that I don't think that I have any old American currency, and that the new bills spend just as well as the old ones do—and contains the exact same value.

Buddha Park, which contains dozens of Buddha statues, serves as a stark reminder that not everyone in the world adheres to the Christian faith

But he still wouldn't have it, so, utilizing the soft light from the security guard's flashlight as he stood too closely, looming over me like a soldier, I dug frantically around in my wallet to retrieve another "old" ten-dollar bill.

Buddha relaxes, seemingly unfazed by the noise and clamber which takes place by the construction cranes in the background, as the city adds more attractions

The driver's white teeth glinted in the gleam of the flashlight as he grabbed for my ragged old currency and flashed a quick smile. And just like that, our little predicament had been resolved.

If all the problems I have ever encountered in my life could have been as easily fixed as simply handing someone tired, old currency, I would be poorer and less seasoned at negotiating and resolving conflicts. (Full disclosure, I have developed a partiality to crisp new bills in my wallet, guess that makes me a typical American).

After completing our check-in that night, Jeffrey and I marveled at the poor condition of our hotel room. The window was cracked, and we could hear the distant yet pervasive sound of churning motorbikes as they navigated the narrow streets below. You see here in Laos the traffic wasn't the only thing that we could hear buzzing. The mosquitos were in on the action, too, in hot pursuit of the blood of American tourists, it seemed.

Trying to look on the bright side, I reluctantly stated, "Well, at least we aren't sleeping out beside the road or in a field somewhere. Those mosquitos are tough tonight." And with that, our exhausted minds and bodies shut down for a night of rest in the buzzing city of Vientiane.

A stray dog grabs a few hurried bites as he begins his morning

The following morning, we woke up early and enjoyed a traditional Asian breakfast which was served at our hotel. We then walked out in the street, to explore for a while. Bands of wandering dogs, with breakfast still very much on their minds, circled the upset trash cans

A French-inspired monument draws many tourists to the site in Vientiane, the capital of Laos

A motorbike driver conducts an early morning delivery to the temple

At a prominent temple in Laos, a statue of an elephant bows to an assortment of statues

Before the temple areas swell with foot traffic, a motorbike driver cruises around the large complex during early morning

which occupied the dusty streets. They feasted on whatever they could find from the trash, and thankfully did not bother us as we sneaked past them, careful to avoid disturbing the most important meal of the day for them.

Later that day, with the sun beating down furiously, we chose to play it cool and relax in an air-conditioned car as we enjoyed a short forty-five-minute drive to visit several exquisite temples and palaces in Vientiane, the capital city of Laos.

There was no shortage of statues and idols erected throughout the city, each representing an important role or figure of the Buddhist or Hindu religion. Quite a few of the figures were significantly disfigured— initially and intentionally so— it seemed. We wished to be as respectful as we could while approaching people who practiced these religions, since we were only guests who had been permitted, albeit briefly, to visit their country. We were honored and privileged to observe their unique practices, daily habits, and cultures.

Perhaps my world had been quite small prior to my leaving my home country for these distinctly unique Asian destinations, because several times I witnessed things which I hadn't known existed in this modern day and age. One example; in Indonesia, I saw on multiple occasions, a procession of worshippers approaching various statues and offering them food. The food looked amazingly delicious however, I am sure that the stony statues never partook in any of the food that was so extravagantly laid out before them that day. The fowl of the air probably swooped down on occasion and snuck portions of the tasty treats as the day progressed.

Even though Laos had been the poorest country I visited in my life, I seemed to enjoy my time there quite well. The thing which I found to be the least pleasant as well as considerably disconcerting, was the air quality here. It was bad. So bad, in fact, that we requested disposable masks from the concierge before we struck out on any lengthy hikes throughout the city.

Exquisite detail and captivating concepts are employed during the construction of ornate temples such as this one in Laos

Glittering like diamonds in the morning sun, intricate temples beckon to curious tourists

Masks are an important accessory here, even for police officers

You see, here in Laos as well as parts of Malaysia, Thailand, Cambodia, and Vietnam, the stench of human waste can be enveloping. This is especially true when walking along a street which smells distinctly like you were trapped inside a sewer plant. I am not even kidding. Here, you will want something to cover your nose, even if you think that you will look silly (and sissy) if you wear a blue mask over your face to keep the most intense offending breezes at arm's length.

Throughout our tour of impoverished Laos, we traveled through a region of the country where a high concentration of Buddhists monks

Orange robes dry on a clothesline outside a temple

Perhaps one of the most iconic scenes in Vientiane, a statue depicting a sleeping Buddha draws large crowds daily

spent their days. Each morning, before the first streaks of light color the eastern sky, the monks jump into their small boats and paddle across the shallow Mekong River, where locals and tourists await them. The monks live on the other side of the river, and perform their watery trek early each morning, crossing the river in search of food from the generous locals.

In this specific area of Laos, the monks fully rely on the donated food which the waiting tourists and locals shower them with. Most of the locals ascribe to Buddhism, and much like Christians, the Buddhists consider it to be in bad taste—as well as unacceptable—to turn your back on a hungry person. In this manner, the locals line up along the riverbanks, bearing food which the monks will then graciously accept and take back to their side of the river.

Even ambulances require a bit of a push sometimes

I understood that whatever food which the monks were given that morning, that is all the food which they will have that day, since they do not go out in search of additional food throughout the day, but rather rely solely on whatever portions they received that morning.

After Jeffrey and I had seen more than our quota of statues, temples, palaces, and various other interesting monuments, we headed back to our heavily guarded hotel. We never did figure out why some hotels throughout Asia were so intensely fortified. We speculated that the police presence might have been serving as a deterrent to the locals, in order to dissuade them from entering the property in their persistent attempts to sell their various wares to the tourists. Or perhaps it was because there had been incidences of crime within the immediate areas of which we traveled.

Our American minds surmised that it was probably just business as usual here, though. "It is probably always like this," I offered. At least that is what I hoped would be the accurate assumption, because shortly thereafter I had an unsettling situation present itself alongside a busy portion of the town at an ATM which I visited.

In need of some Lao cash, I had stopped at an ATM and was occupied with attempting to complete my transaction, when suddenly a creepy feeling swept over me, like I was being watched. I understand that ATMs are outfitted with cameras and can observe and record your every move. But this feeling that burrowed deeper and deeper within me grew more and more real. Averting my steady gaze from the brightly lit screen, I glanced around, becoming cognizant of my entire surroundings.

My eyes scoped the area and discovered nothing unusual. Until something glinted inside the abandoned storefront window which was located directly in front of me, no less than ten feet. I don't think that I will ever forget what I saw next. There, sitting stalwartly on a chair immediately inside the window, was a Lao police officer, armed to the teeth and sporting military fatigues. I think I might have flinched. In fact, I know I did.

Wanting to appear unstartled, I nodded my head and smiled at him, convincingly trying to play the part of the friendly tourist that I was. He returned my smile and nodded, shifting his weight. The glint which I had seen moments earlier through the window had been the sunlight glancing off his incredibly intimidating gun.

Customers are slow in parting with their money early in the morning, as this fellow can attest

I quickly looked down at the ATM. Piles of colorful Lao cash were sitting there, waiting on me. My card had worked, once more. With my transaction complete, I grabbed the fistful of money and left the area faster than I had approached it.

Not wanting to be bothered with pesky little life details or tasks such as doing laundry, Jeffrey and I had inquired earlier that morning about the possibility of our hotel doing our laundry for us. The staff there had agreed upon performing the task for us needy American boys. This allowed us access to a more relaxed, spontaneous day filled with fun vacation things.

After dropping our laundry at the counter, we walked to a nearby marketplace and mingled with the locals, negotiating prices which had been set sky high for us 'tourists,' or so it seemed. On our return trip, we passed by a laundry and dry-cleaning facility. And by facility, I mean a ramshackle shack.

"Here's a laundry service," Jeffrey exclaimed. "We could have just brought our laundry here, it's so close to our hotel."

Indeed, this shack was in proximity to our super fancy hotel. The two buildings were in stark contrast to each other, even though they were located no more than two-hundred-feet apart. "Yes, we should have brought our clothes here," I replied. "This place does look really interesting."

A few electric washers were lined up on the dirt floor along the side of the small tent-like building. Brightly colored clothing hung on several wash lines which had been strung outside and was drying in the hot summer sun. The air was laden with the pleasing scent of fresh laundry. It seemed as if no one occupied the small business, so Jeffery and I began to walk away.

We hadn't completely turned around to leave before my eyes caught sight of a haggard-looking, exhausted lady. But that wasn't what had caught Jeffery's eye.

The clothing which appeared mysteriously on a clothesline a few blocks from the hotel

"Hey Leroy, these are our clothes!" he exclaimed incredulously. "Come here and take a look at this."

"Of course, these aren't our clothes," I quickly retorted. And then, with a hint of indignance showing in my voice, I added. "We left our laundry at our hotel, or did you forget?"

As I hurried over to the line of clothes which he was standing beside I immediately saw that he had been correct. There were our clothes, neatly hanging in the sun, dangling from plastic hangars. This was truly baffling to me.

A distinctly unique pulley system is in place on a construction site in Vientiane

Attempting to strike up a conversation with the weary lady, I asked her how she got ahold of our clothes, since we had left them at our hotel just a few hours earlier. But our conversation wasn't meant to be, since she couldn't understand a word of English. In exasperation, she waved her hands at us, indicating that we can't be here, or, more likely, that we weren't supposed to be seeing

A motorbike is left lying in the middle of a street after its owner was involved in an accident

A woman sits contentedly at her food stall located outside the city of Phnom Penh

When business is slow, a cellphone comes in handy to distract from the cares of the world

A young boy assists his father with the steering as they maneuver through the city streets

what we were seeing.

"But these are my clothes, I can't just leave them here," I protested. Also wishing to be obedient, we turned on our heels and walked away, reluctantly leaving our clothes behind on the line. As we made our way back to

Construction sites in Laos, including this one, are an indication of what it looks like to have inadequate safety procedures in place

our hotel, I glanced back one final time at my drying clothes. Would I ever see them again? And just how exactly had that lady gotten access to our laundry?

Eager to help with the general labor consisting of constructing a garage, a young lad lifts an object in order to assist the crew

An abandoned rickshaw sits along a crumbling city block in Laos

Construction of another temple is underway in Vientiane, Laos

An established restaurant beside a busy street outside Siem Reap

An emaciated cow glances absentmindedly into the distance

Fancy figures are placed at the entrance to the temple

Peculiar rides abound throughout the Cambodian cities

The usual fare offered at various food stalls throughout Cambodia

The alleyway which housed the hotel that the author stayed at

The ingenuity of Cambodians can hardly be measured, especially regarding their creativity within the motorbike and trailer industry

Several colorful rickshaws await to transport potential clients

Wheelbarrows, similar to this one, are used prevalently in Cambodia for various construction projects

Piercing the skies with a majestic white pillar, this palace appears quite presidential

CHAPTER 10
FLOATING VILLAGES ON THE MURKY MEKONG

A bird flies overhead as a slight breeze rustles the plastic covering the sides of the villagers' homes

The stress of laundry day finally dissipated late that night when the phone in our hotel room rang. It was the front desk, informing us that our laundry was ready to be picked up. Jeffery and I used the solo elevator at the end of the hall and collected our belongings.

"Here is your laundry, sir," the well-suited hotel manager cheerfully announced as he saw us approaching the desk.

The clean contents within the neatly wrapped clear plastic bag was a welcome sight. Believe me, if there are several things which I have learned throughout this trip, on top of the list of lessons learned would be the priceless pleasure of having clean laundry to wear. It seems like such a simple thing, but when there are no coin laundry facilities to be found along your journey through the Asian countryside, it doesn't take long to fully appreciate such basics.

Sometimes, we had the opportunity to wash our clothes in the tub in our hotel room and resorted to hanging our wet clothes on the balcony (whenever our room had such amenities) to dry in the sun. However, we were mindful of how and when we did this, because in some of the Asian countries which we traveled through, it was considered very offensive to hang underwear out on the line, especially if it would be visible to any passerby. There were signs which stated that such types of laundry are supposed to be dried inside the room, or at least out of sight.

We never did tell our hotel manager that we had caught on to their little game. The poor lady which we had seen down the street had been tasked with washing all the hotel patrons' laundry, each day, seven days a week. Initially, I pitied her, but then I realized that the hotel was truly going above and beyond in delegating tasks and providing the community with much-needed work. By subcontracting the laundry services to the neighbor lady down the street from the fancy hotel, it provided the poorer residents with hopefully adequate income. Not only that, it had given the lady a sense of purpose.

We arrived in Cambodia, our next stop, on an exceptionally hot summer day. The heat broiled off the tarmac as we scurried across like rats, eager to escape the intense rays of the brutal sun. It was 107 degrees Fahrenheit, and when out in the direct sun, the temperature

Basic buildings are cluttered with trash along the riverbanks

seemed to surpass that.

We thought we had seen poor, impoverished districts while in Laos, and in all reality, this was true. But here in the outskirts

Children play with a ball along the parched, dusty edges of the riverbank

of Siem Reap, we were in for a surprise. The community hospital was besieged with overgrowth—tall grass and bushes greedily claimed the space surrounding the hospital grounds. Several emaciated cows were hungrily munching on the few areas of shrubs and grass which

Clusters of mangroves persisted along the riverbanks throughout the tour of the floating village

Sheep and goats graze on the sparse grasses along the riverbanks

could be seen immediately in front of the hospital's main entrance. The sight— in itself— seemed to be totally unreal to disbelieving American eyes.

While the taxi driver navigated the crowded streets during a late Monday

Muddy waves are created as a boat expeditiously transports several tourists to the mainland

afternoon, Jeffrey and I gazed out the dust-covered window of the car, totally engrossed by the scenes which passed us by. It seemed as if we just glided past extremely needy people, as they sat or stood outside their small stick houses which were wrapped in plastic around the sides and featured rusted sheet metal for their roofs. Many of the roofs outside the city were bedecked with old rubber tires, which held down the loose sheet metal, which obviously no one had bothered to fasten with screws.

The air was thick with smoke, it seemed as if everyone was burning

Rubber tires are tossed haphazardly onto the sheet metal roofs

Cows dare to venture into the dusty streets

trash or roasting ears of unhusked corn and chestnuts. A few cows dared to wander into the street directly in front of our vehicle, but our skilled driver deftly maneuvered his rickshaw around the aimless animals. Several monkeys, playing around in the pineapple and banana trees, jumped from branch to branch, appearing unaware of the scores of cars and humans who occupied the dusty streets below.

Poverty appeared to envelop us, and with long, bony fingers, threatened to push its way into the windows of the car, forcing me to not only behold the sights but to feel and understand. Though the car

A family of monkeys dawdles in the shade to escape the summer sun

Homes fashioned from pieces of plastic and sticks are prevalent along the banks of the Mekong River in Siem Reap

A little boy plays alone in a boat outside his family's riverbank home

window served as a make-believe barrier between the haves (us) and the have-nots (them), I couldn't imagine living in such an impoverished manner.

It was an eye-opening experience for me to witness

As children play along the banks, multiple gulls soar through the skies above

Rudimentary walkways provide ease of access to the waters of the Mekong River

the considerable poverty and daily struggles which some people on the planet really go through every day. For them, this level of poverty was nearly inescapable and perhaps, at least to them, seemingly insurmountable. You see, I was going to go home again, real soon, to my home country, where nearly everyone, including the Amish and Mennonites, lived very comfortable lives. I had already booked a flight which would whisk me from this poverty in just a few short days. Living in squalor was a foreign concept to me, personally. And for that, I again felt incredibly guilty.

I began asking myself some questions for which I could not produce effective, accurate answers. Why had I been born in America anyway, and not in a terribly poor country? How is it that some countries and regions in the world are subjected to seemingly endless cycles of poverty and malnourishment? Why did God, in his infinite wisdom, choose to bless me so richly? Perhaps, an abundance of material blessing aren't actually blessings at all, rather stumbling blocks?

These were difficult questions. But I was glad to entertain them as we passed slowly through

Villagers of various ages rush around to conduct repairs on a nearby boat

the most poverty-stricken areas of Cambodia. I wished to remain mindful of these poor, needy souls.

Now that I have painted a bit of a picture of what life is like for some people on the other side of the world, you would certainly be inclined to assume that the people here wore sad, hopeless looks on their faces, right?

But they didn't. In fact, nearly everyone I met throughout the four-days which I spent there, had million-dollar smiles plastered on their dust-streaked faces. Everyone seemed genuinely happy with their lot in life.

I had to wonder; if everything were suddenly taken away from me, my material possessions, etc., would I even have the courage and strength to smile? If I were to lose everything I owned—which really isn't that much—but a whole lot more than these people will ever own in several lifetimes, would I then count that personal loss as a great adversity? Would I rejoice in losing everything? Would I even come close to worshipping and praising God in a manner akin to which the Bible tells us Job had done during his great loss? I am afraid I know—all too well—the answer to these questions, unfortunately, and it does stir a distinctly uncomfortable feeling within the walls of my heart.

That evening, after we had become adequately introduced to life within the broken walls of the dust-filled, motorbike deluged city, we scheduled a river boat tour to a floating village. Everyone here referred to the area which we were going to as a 'floating village.'

Due to the language barrier of our tour guide, I am unsure if these floating houses and various other structures are actually floating buildings, per se, or if the structures are built on stilts and then simply engulfed with waters during the wet season. We had visited during the dry season, so that logic doesn't seem to hold much water, either. However, we were told it is a permanently floating village, and I wasn't about to argue.

We glided down the murky Mekong River for nearly an hour, as dusk became increasingly apparent. Trees began to cast long, shadowy figures across the waters, and the branches appeared to represent the malnourished arms of a dreadful creature. Trying to outrace the

A family navigates the muddy waterways after they complete a few purchases at a floating market in Cambodia

A rush of boats make their way toward the entrance of the floating village

rapidly setting sun, the captain of our small motorboat hit the throttle and black smoke from the engine was thrust high into the evening sky.

We reached the floating village as the remaining streaks of light paraded across the sky. Introducing us to the unique village, a local pointed out where the police station was located, as well as the prison. There was also a convenience store, a school for orphans, a church, and a bank which comprised the floating village. Of course, there were also numerous houses within the village.

Our guide began to share at length about life here within the floating village. "Here at the school, the little children have no mommy or daddy," he remarked, thoughtfully. "They never leave the school. This school is their home. They have no home to go to, no parents, nobody

The floating school for orphans

that cares for them. Except here. Here, they have a place to live. Every day, the village people, they bring food to the school on their boats."

The children play inside the school and on the porch, whenever they have completed their academic requirements. A police station is located within proximity to the school, and so is the prison. Our guide continued to explain that if anyone commits a minor crime, they are locked up within the village prison. "Any residents of the floating village who is found guilty of high

A police station

crimes, they are transported by boat where they are then sent to a prison on the mainland," he remarked matter-of-factly.

According to the guide, most of the people living here in this watery village never leave their houses to go to the mainland. When I dutifully inquired why not, the guide kindly yet emphatically reiterated. "They live here. This is their home. Understand?"

Well, in all fairness, I had been trying to understand. But to me, it was all such a foreign concept, and somewhat difficult to wrap my mind around the fact that there are people who had constructed houses

A young man flashes a victory sign as their boat continues along the Mekong River

and lived permanently on the murky waters of the rippling Mekong.

Darkness beckoned like a persistent cancer, and we indicated to our guide that we wished to return

Boys are taught at a young age to safely operate their passenger boats

to the area where our driver was waiting for us. On the return trip, we saw numerous motorboats, each in a rudimental state, operated by young boys. These lads had just completed a day's work, which consisted largely of transporting tourists to the floating village from the mainland. Their broad smiles were priceless as they waved eagerly to Jeffery and I who had been sitting on the ledge of the small boat which we occupied. It was evident that they had enjoyed

Young men enjoy a few relaxed moments on their boat before they transport more tourists to the floating village

their day and were eager to return home to their families for the evening.

One thing which consistently appeared quite evident to us, was the impressive work ethic of these Cambodians. Here, even the young people were employed, busy with something. Some of the youth, barely able to see above the windshields of the cars, transported tourists to their destinations. Still others operated motorbikes at a relatively young age, delivering food and vegetables to various street markets. It seemed as if the Cambodians, Vietnamese, and Lao folks had honed their skills and had seized a work ethic akin to the Amish and Mennonites. Granted, being born an Amish or Mennonite doesn't entail that we will not find a poor, nearly non-existent, work ethic in some people within that community, but my point

Dragging his nets beside him, a man maneuvers through the muddy waters as a young boy swims close-by

is, slothfulness tends to not easily be tolerated within these communities, in much the same manner as these poor, hard-working Asians seemed to value a strong, vibrant work ethic within

Intent on catching a fish or two, this man has no qualms of immersing himself into the murky waters of the Mekong River

their families and their respective communities.

Late that evening, upon the conclusion of our river tour, we stopped briefly to wander aimlessly around a lotus farm. Water lilies grew beautifully around the picturesque Cambodian farm, and swarms of mosquitos followed us for the duration of our quick tour.

The lotus plant produces a seed which, the driver told us, is used for medicinal and health-related purposes by the villagers living on the

All smiles, a friendly group of motorists waves hello

farm and surrounding city dwellers. Numerous straw huts, strategically aligned throughout the property, created an ethereal scene as twinkling lights danced in a most hypnotic manner across the slow-moving waters of the nearby water hole.

That night, exhausted from the heat and the excitement of the memorable Mekong River

Clutching precariously to its sister, a small child appears lost in thought while watching as the traffic passes them by

tour, I laid my head on my pillow and fondly replayed the scenes of the day within my mind. Even though I was exhausted, I couldn't stop thinking about the staggering poverty and the wealthy smiles which I had

A tired motorike driver grabs a quick cat nap

witnessed that day. And neither should I want to. Moments such as these will surely be tucked away far into the deepest corners of my heart for a long time.

I am still trying to understand how it is possible for people with so little—seemingly nothing—to be so incredibly happy. Much happier, even, then you or me.

Feeling playful, a young boy puts his climbing skills to the test while his friends continue to engage in conversation

Lotus farms such as this one can be found throughout Cambodia

Rice straw covers the roofs of several huts located on a Cambodian lotus farm

A boat appears lost as it remains moored outside the floating village

A largely unused boat rests along the Mekong River

A man pauses to check his cell phone while working on an irrigation system

A scene of desolation and serenity, all wrapped in one confusing package

A uniquely outfitted piece of farming equipment sets outside a village in Siem Reap

Children pause briefly before crossing a crowded city street in Vientiane, Laos

Amid a kaleidoscope of colors, a man carefully attends to his boat

As heavy earthmoving equipment stirs in the background, children play in the mud with empty soda bottles along the banks of the murky Mekong

An empty structure sets along the banks of the Mekong River

As the remaining streaks of light fade from the hazy skies, a few farmers attempt to conduct repairs on an irrigation system.

Church services are held in this building on a weekly basis

Clothes hang on the line outside a home near Siem Reap's city center

Colorful boats converge along the banks of the muddied river and contrast sharply with the murky waters

Containers filled with petrol which will be used to power the boats' engines, are unloaded near the banks of the river

Engines dangle dutifully from their posts near the banks of the river

Enjoying a brief break from work, a boat operator and his watercraft lounge in proximity of a busy excavator

Selling various items is an essential means of survival in Cambodia. Here, a girl braids her younger sister's hair while they await potential customers at their vegetable market

Irrigation systems clog the main artery as hundreds of boats pass by the area daily

Laborers attempt to construct an addition to an existing floating building

Large modern equipment muddies the waters near the banks of the Mekong River as primitive motorboats pass by in a flash

Looking on in an intent manner, a girl observes a few children playing

Majority of Cambodians living in the countryside quickly learn to live on a fraction compared to their city dwelling counterparts

Motorists occupy the dirt roadway atop the river's banks

Resting under the plastic roof of his home, a man enjoys a respite from the summer sun

Several large boats await the throngs of tourists which flood the area each day

While others tend to odd jobs, a young boy enjoys a quick swim in the muddy waters

Sticks protrude from the waters and primitive buildings within the floating village

Small boys wait till tourist boats arrive at the dock, then beg for money as they try to assist the passengers with disembarkation

Strolling along the riverbanks, a young man carries a stick

Teasing in an affectionate manner, a young boy tries to tug a smile from the lips of his friend

The murky waters of the Mekong attracted many waterfowl

These two bask in the soft rays of the evening sun as they head home after a long day of transporting tourists

Vibrant and cheery, boats such as this one make floating along a muddy river appear both practical and enjoyable

Villagers toil outside their homes along the banks of the soiled river

Walking slowly back to his home, a man retires for the day from transporting tourists with his boat

CHAPTER 11
POVERTY AND BEAUTY IN A CAMBODIAN STILT VILLAGE

Cattle scour the landscape anxiously for a few nibbles in a field near Battambang

The day dawned brightly, sizzling with heat even before we had finished eating the last remaining bites of our bacon. This morning, Jeffrey and I ate rice and baked beans once again, but this time, we also jumped at the rare opportunity to indulge in eggs and bacon.

Throughout Asia, the primary countries which we visited had served baked beans and rice as staples for breakfast. It was difficult to adjust to that, but when I eventually subscribed to the mentality that those two foods can technically (but barely) be consumed at the morning meal while walking away with both a satisfied tummy and a portion of my dignity remaining, it wasn't so bad. After all, in some regions of the world, starving humans would rejoice at the thought of beans and rice. Initially, I had felt ungrateful, and reminded myself that my attitude and behavior was selfish and acutely akin to that of the murmuring Israelites in the book of *Numbers*.

"Good Morning. How are you?" a friendly voice greeted us. The voice belonged to our conversational taxi driver who was scheduled to drive us an hour into the country, where we would visit a stilt village.

"We wish to learn all that we can about your people," I explained while finding my seat in the immaculate minivan, which was well-suited for the most finicky of American tourists. "Can you take us to the poorest areas here?" And then, without waiting for his reply, I quickly added, "We wish to see how the Cambodian farmers live and learn how they earn a living."

Wandi, our driver, looked back at us and smiled widely. "This is good to hear," he began. "It makes my heart happy that you want to learn more about my people. I will take you to the poorest village, and then when you are done, I also take you to largest religious site in the world. It's right here in Siem Reap."

I settled back in my seat. It all sounded well and good to me. For the next sixty minutes, I observed the locals as they headed to the vegetable and fruit markets, while others toiled out in

Motorbikes travel in either direction as their occupants pass through the village

their small plots of land as the morning sun flooded them with sunshine. It was the dry season, and no rain had fallen here in weeks, leaving the earth parched and dusty. Some crops had required irrigation in order to grow.

That morning, we crossed over into several districts, each with its own

Motorbikes are employed for a number of purposes throughout SE Asia

A residence in a rural area of Cambodia

unique flavor of buildings and people. The dress throughout Asia remained predominantly respectable, in fact, much more so than in the United States. Even though the temperature soared well over 100 degrees Fahrenheit each day, the natives clothed themselves in a respectable manner.

A resident sits outside as a heavy blanket of dust settles over everything

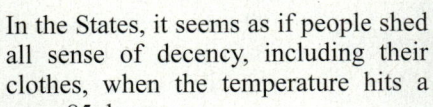

During the wet season, the waters typically rise as high as the stilts

In the States, it seems as if people shed all sense of decency, including their clothes, when the temperature hits a mere 85 degrees.

The car slowed down as we entered

Children walk along a path in the dusty, smoke-filled village

A stilt village located in the poorest regions of Cambodia

A vegetable vendor steadies her motorbike as she passes through the village

the outskirts of our village. "Ok, I will drop you off here, and then I will meet you at the other end of the village," our driver announced.

My heart stopped briefly as I surveyed my surroundings. "No way," I thought to myself. "This wasn't part of the deal. I just wanted to see the village, not be stranded here forever."

But I reluctantly agreed to exit the car and walk through the village, only after I had the driver promise that he wouldn't leave us stranded in the middle of this dusty stilt village in the Cambodian countryside.

Wandi had been wise. In fact, very wise. He knew exactly what kind of experience I had needed before I headed back home to America. Walking through that village, as it turns out, would be one of the best things that ever happened to me. Because I had been asked to trudge

Some children play outside their school while others purchase inexpensive trinkets during recess

A woman prepares food on an open fire

through the dusty village, I had also been forced to witness poverty in the rawest of forms.

The stench of smoke was the first thing to reach my pampered nostrils, followed in rapid succession by the unpleasant odor of sewage and unclean water supplies. Here, images of poverty straight out of *National Geographic,* which I had thought would no longer exist today, came to life. Emaciated, unclothed children played in the abandoned streets, under the watchful gaze of their mothers who fussed over an open-pit fire as they prepared a sparse lunch for their families.

The hum of an occasional motorbike split the otherwise eerie silence, as it slowly passed through this village on its way to the next town. It was, by all accounts, abundantly obvious that not many tourists come here. In retrospect, the village is way off the beaten path for most tourists, no matter how adventurous they are.

I glanced over at Jeffery, who had been walking slowly beside me, eyes glued to his surroundings, observing every little detail of the impoverished village. Through the glum silence, I managed to mutter. "Jeff, I can't possibly be prepared to see more of this. I didn't know places like this still exist in the world."

In truth, I have been aware of poverty-stricken areas throughout the globe. But even if I would have read one-thousand books on these poor regions, nothing,

A motorbike passes by a wedding ceremony which is taking place inside the colorful tent

and I mean nothing, could have adequately prepared me to walk through that village that day.

Until you feel the heavy, red dust clinging to your face, and smell the arid smoke of an open fire, mixed with the doubly revolting stench of human waste, and see the impossibly slender bodies of emaciated livestock and human beings, you simply cannot fathom the realness of the moment.

That moment was a turning point for me. I was so incredibly grateful to Wandi for encouraging us to walk through the village. For it was there, in that Cambodian stilt village, that I met some of the most inspiring, amazing human beings.

When we had reached the edge of the village, Jeffrey and I expressed our desire to visit the monastery and school that was also located within the village. The friendly, quiet monks were all too eager to meet us, and permitted us to browse through their living

The daily duties surrounding a monk's lifestyle are rather relaxed during the hottest part of the summer

quarters. It was a simple life, for sure. Raw wooden planks covered the earthen floor, and cheap cots were lined along the walls. The building was primitive and lacked enclosure on either side, allowing easy access to the outside.

Sweeping the temple steps and surrounding areas is a task performed daily throughout the villages

Cambodian students leave their footwear on the steps of their school

Small schools such as this one can be found in the deepest pockets of the countrysides

Three scholars clasp each other's hands as they prepare to enter the classroom

The largest room was rather dark, even throughout the day, since the building lacked electricity. The rays of the sun snuck through a slit in the rusted metal roof and illuminated a small corner of the otherwise gloomy room. I am unsure which shone the brightest; the wide smiles of the monks as they proudly pulled back the curtain of their quiet lifestyle, providing me with a glimpse into their unique lives, or the jagged crack in the roof where the sun peaked through.

Time seemed to slip away while I was lost, deep in thought, here in the village. It seemed all so far removed from the bustling lifestyles which we lead in Lancaster County, Pennsylvania. Sure, horse and buggies travel slowly on the secondary roads which slice through the most idyllic portions of Lancaster County, but here in the dry rice fields and emotionally moving monasteries of Cambodia, life seems to move at an even slower pace than that.

Well, it was time to bid farewell to the monks and see what the schoolchildren were learning, so we walked approximately five-hundred-feet to the entrance of the schoolhouse. The school was also off-grid and was rather dark inside. The sunlight which found its way through the cloudy windows was much appreciated by the scholars, of this I am sure.

Jeffery and I had purchased a sizable stack of coloring books and pencils before we entered the school. We paused outside the open door of the school and asked the teacher if it would be all right if we sat in as visitors for a bit. We explained that we are from America, and that we attended a small parochial school, not entirely unlike this one, and would be honored if we could observe for a spell.

The young lady eagerly obliged, immediately offering us a warm smile. Her English wasn't the best, so our dialogue was somewhat limited. Throughout the conversation though, we determined that she had been tasked with the responsibility of teaching between thirty and forty young boys and girls, all whom resided within the small village.

The curriculum seemed very relaxed and casual. Colorful posters lined the white walls of the dimly lit room, which I had assumed were art assignments which the scholars had completed. Shortly upon our entrance into the school, the little scholars began to sing a song in what I assumed was their native Cambodian language. After they were done singing, the teacher requested that I distribute the books and pencils to each of the students.

Visiting a Cambodian school was a learning experience for the author and his nephew

The scholars couldn't have been more gracious. Clasping their hands together in much the same manner as we do when we pray, they individually proclaimed their thanks with a soft "Thank You, Sir!" the moment I presented them with a book or pencil. The smiles on their faces I will never forget. It had been such a small, inexpensive gesture on my part, but it seemed as if it had meant the world to them. I wish to remember to exercise such a thankful heart and prayerful attitude whenever I receive something, no matter how small, from someone.

It is difficult for many to grasp the enormity of the complex

A balloon glides through the smoky air above Ankor Wat

After stopping briefly for a refreshing ice cream treat along the way to Angkor Wat, our next attraction, we observed several monkeys as they vied for our attention. The playful moneys had jumped up on the hood of a parked taxi car and were pulling

A majestic religious site in Siem Reap which was built hundreds of years ago

Imagine the vast amounts of physical labor involved which obviously encompassed a project such as this

Intricate stonework surrounds the site and visually appeals to many tourists

on the wipers, allowing them to snap back onto the windshield. They continued their antics, greatly relishing in the attention we gave them. The sharp, cracking sound of the wipers hitting against the windshield also seemed to fill them with a sense of excitement.

The vast area which we were now visiting is considered the largest religious site in the world. Millions of tourists from all over the globe flood the area each year, which has become a Unesco World Heritage Site.

Angkor Wat is a remarkably expansive site which features acres and acres of historic, religious monuments and ruins. It is widely speculated by historians that majority of the monuments which are still standing there today were built throughout the first half of the twelfth century. The site

The well-known tourist attraction features crumbling statues constructed between the 12th and 13th centuries

is also considered as one of the most preserved architectural masterpieces on the planet.

The funerary-themed temples and monuments are artfully and tastefully designed, sparing absolutely no attention to detail. Meticulous architecture towers high into the sky, and spans the sprawling, five-hundred-acre rectangular area.

It had surely been a busy yet wonderful day. Perhaps it was even the best day of the trip so far. I think it very well might have been. At any rate, it was here in Cambodia that I called a close friend of mine and told him that I had run into a bit of trouble during my stay here.

You see, in a few short days I was planning to leave the country. And I really didn't want to leave. It hurt physically when I considered leaving these friendly, wonderful people in the rearview mirror of my taxi.

I believe it felt wrong to pack my luggage and jump on that plane, since these impoverished people whom I had just briefly met had taught me so much about life. I honestly felt as though they had taught me more about the fundamentals of life within these few short days than what I could have possibly taught them in an entire year.

But goodbye it must be. I couldn't linger much longer. I learned that sometimes goodbyes can be the hardest part of traveling.

Vehicles pass under a lofty gate as dust collects at the edges of the country road

Uniquely shaped trees flank the aging religious site

The entrance to a religious site looms high in the distance

A shimmering temple constructed immediately outside the stilt village

Wearing a t-shirt with an image of an American flag, a young girl pushes her bicycle along the dirt road

A bike mechanic washes a bicycle outside his shop

A child and an adult monk sit on the steps of a rudimental building along a rural road

A friendly girl, dressed for a wedding she attended, runs beside a taxi the author occupied in hopes she can share a treat with the Americans

A high school is placed on stilts, and during the wet season, the students arrive daily in boats instead of bikes

A ladder provides hours of fun for a young Cambodian boy

A market located in proximity of the revered Ankor Wat religious site

A primate feeds her young under the shade of a nearby tree

A shy girl poses for a photograph outside her classroom

Wagons constructed of bamboo sides are a dime a dozen in rural areas

A vendor and his assistants navigate the crowded city streets

A young boy emerges from a residence located within the stilt village

A young child clings precariously from the porch while observing the menfolk below

An emaciated cow rummages for a bite to eat

Bicycles are a primary source of transportation within the village during the dry season

Boats are used as a primary source of travel during the wet season

Children play along the dusty road which passes through the stilt village

Colorful toy trucks, similar to those found in North American, are spotted within the impoverished village

Dogs and humans alike benefit from a respite from the day's demanding itinerary

Dogs and roosters compete with humans for a bite to eat at a local eatery

During the wet season, the waters will rise, providing ease of access for the numerous boats within the village

Houses are basic and lack any luxuries in the stilt village

Houses are placed on stilts in villages which are subject to high waters during the wet season

Laundry hangs on the line as a man waves hello to passersby while relaxing in the lower area of the stilt house

Many boats are colorful and possess a cheery disposition

Most petrol stations also sell various trinkets and necessities

Motorists operate interesting vehicles on the city streets

Muddy waters prevail as a man occupies the shallows while wielding a basket and net

Observing from a branch, these two seemed to be slightly amused by their human visitors

Pausing briefly on their journey, a family purchases a few items from a vendor deep in the countryside

Pieces of plastic serve as a sun shield for a country motorist

Pushing her bicycles through the smoke-choked village, a woman wears a hat to shield herself from the rays of the sun

Residences in rural areas are furnished with only the bare necessities

Seizing every opportunity to make a sale, a young lad cruises around on his bicycle
while attempting to sell bottles of water

Sweeping the dusty street seemed futile, however, was a common scene throughout the country

Vehicles such as these are commonplace throughout the Cambodian countrysides

Vendors of various wares are prevalent along the Cambodian village streets

CHAPTER 12
REFLECTIONS IN A VIETNAMESE SALT FIELD

Waters reflect beautifully at the foot of a monument in Battambang

It's soon time to jump on a plane to Vietnam, but while we are waiting here in the departure terminal, I want to share a quick story with you.

While Jeffrey and I were in Cambodia, we spent a lot of time in the back seats of a less-than-optimal taxi. We considered ourselves fortunate enough that the car was equipped with air conditioning, however, that is about where the luxury ended.

Needing a short break from being subjected to the bumpy, dusty country roads within Siem Reap, we requested, somewhat adamantly, that our driver stop as soon as we enter the town or a market, so that we could relax a bit while we enjoy a fresh coffee. You would think that with such a high temperature of 100 degrees, that the first thing on our minds would be ice cream. Well, we also wanted that, too.

Our minds had become quite dull by mid-day, since we had been required to leave the comfortable confines of our hotel room early that morning—at 3:30 AM—to catch a ride to the village which we wished to see.

The car slowed to a stop when we arrived at the first market on the way back to our hotel. After some simple detective work, I sniffed out a great café which served wonderful espressos. Or so I thought.

As we walked up to the counter, we were kindly greeted by the friendly proprietor. We placed our orders and paid for our beverages, being careful to avoid leaving any tip, since tipping is considered unnecessary and even offensive in most Asian

The power source which was responsible for brewing double espressos for Jeffrey and the author

countries. The man took our money and told us to please be seated. Then he walked out to the sidewalk and down the street for a few steps.

I initially thought to myself, "Hey, come back here. You can't possibly know how badly I need an espresso right now."

But instead, I watched as he walked over to an old belt-and-pulley situation which was located not too far from his café. After hand-cranking the antiquated engine three times, the old thing sprung to life, depositing a cloud of thick, black smoke into the already filthy air.

A few minutes after the engine had sputtered to life, my espresso was served to me in a fancy white cup, as fresh as could be. I smiled and asked the man if I may take a few photographs of his interesting power source. He graciously obliged and laughed heartily when I told him that no coffee shop in the United States has such a unique source of power.

Don't worry, our flight is delayed by only thirty minutes, so I have time for one more quick story of Cambodia. Perhaps I should have titled this chapter *The Cambodian Chronicles*.

We had quite a few taxi drivers while we were in Cambodia; some of them excellent and one of them awful. I believe, had you been with us, that you would agree with my description. You see, I am unsure if we spent more time bouncing around on the shoulder of the dusty highway or on the actual driving lane of the roadway itself. At any rate, we were continually clipping by at a decent rate of speed, considering the poor road conditions.

Within the course of eight hours—yes, it was an incredibly long day—our driver nearly hit four motorbikes. Now, this might not sound bad yet, but remember that our car is traveling erratically at a speed of 55 mph, and so are the motorbikes. The most harrowing information of this hair-raising account is that three of the motorbikes which our driver nearly hit while we were racing down the roadway were occupied by families with little children. None of them were wearing helmets.

Needless to say, it would have been a very bad scenario had our driver indeed hit them, especially since the nearest legitimate trauma center was located within the neighboring country. Jeffrey and I were very displeased and felt unsafe, even while inside his car, for the duration of the eight-hour round trip. It was a long day of nail-biting for me. When we finally arrived safely at our destination that night, Jeffrey announced that he would hold our driver responsible for his first gray hairs which he was sure had sprouted that very day.

Ok, that is enough of reminiscing; the boarding gate has now opened, let's head off on our next adventure.

From the list of countries that we previously visited, Vietnam proved to be the most challenging and intense. Shortly after our plane touched down, we were required to wait for approximately thirty minutes at the immigration booth before we were permitted to officially enter the country. The questions which most international travelers are required to answer are vast and encompassing, ranging from what our religion is, the address and name of the place where we work, the names, birthdates, and addresses of our brothers and sisters, as well as our phone numbers.

It all seemed a bit excessive, since we had more-or-less breezed through the immigration and customs lines in other airports. After waiting for about thirty minutes, the officials finally returned our passports and permitted us entry into the country.

Prior to our admittance, it seemed likely that it might be problematic that we identified as Christians on our immigration form. But then my thoughts went to an oft-repeated phrase I had heard from several ministers: *If you were arrested for being a Christian, would there be enough evidence to convict you?*

I thought about that for a while. For a few more moments, I continued pondering upon that, kicking those thoughts around in my head. I hoped that there would be enough evidence to convict me.

The streets of Ho Chi Minh City, formally known as Saigon, were buzzing with motorbikes. We had thought we saw, in Indonesia, the maximum number of motorbikes that could possibly be squeezed into one lane of traffic. But here in Vietnam, it seemed as if they rewrote the laws of pragmatism. Yes, they very likely did, because you couldn't possibly otherwise pack more motorbikes into a single area than what they did here.

Suffice it to say that there aren't any emissions enforcements here, and the streets baked under the sun in a heavy haze of spent petrol. As we walked along the broken, chipped sidewalks, our eyes caught a glimpse of something quite extraordinary. We stopped to investigate.

In the middle of the sidewalk, sat a

Coffee grounds dry in the sun along a sidewalk in Vietnam

wooden tray filled with used coffee grounds. The tray had been placed in a sun-soaked area, and we assumed that the grounds were being dried for a specific purpose.

A man was relaxing in a cheap plastic lawn chair close by, so we asked him why a tray of coffee grounds would be blocking pedestrians' access along the sidewalk. His English was very poor, but he tried to explain that the dried coffee grounds would be scattered to the roots of a nearby tree. I am not sure if I believe that, because the few times that I ordered coffee here in Vietnam, it tasted distinctly burnt and dreadful, which leads me to believe that even the coffee grounds get reused here.

A Vietnamese tailor smiles as he demonstrates his work

Later that afternoon, we chatted with another man who sat behind a barely operable foot-pedal sewing machine. He explained, as best he could, that he has been sitting here at the same spot for more than twenty years, each day conducting emergency tailor repairs for men and women. His friend was sitting beside him and asked us if our clothes

Everyone needs a break from work occasionally

are needful of any tailoring or alterations, that he could perform adjustments on the spot. We thanked him for explaining and since our clothes weren't ripped from the tiger den which we had visited while in Thailand, we were, thankfully, in no need of a tailor's services.

The Vietnamese are a hard-working people, and this was most notable when we embarked on two early morning excursions throughout the countryside. One morning, before the clock had chimed four times, Jeffrey and I woke up early so that we could tour a working rice field, located about an hour outside the city of Na Trang.

As the lights from our taxi car cut through the early morning darkness, which was cloaked in a thick summer haze, we noticed that there were large numbers of people working through the night. Or than they had been starting their day super early, I am not sure which.

Repairs are a constant with aging farming equipment in Cambodia

Motorbikes were beginning to fill the streets, unloading fresh vegetables and meats at the scores of street markets. Still other residents were washing windows, cleaning their motorbikes, wiping down food stalls, or sleeping on the bikes. Yes, more than six people, who looked as if they might have been working the entire night, perhaps making food deliveries, etc., were spotted sleeping on the seats of their motorbikes which were parked precariously along the curves of the increasingly busy streets.

After we drove a bit farther into the countryside, we saw several more people sleeping in hammocks beside their vegetable and petrol roadside stalls. Throughout Asia, it is not uncommon to see random roadside stalls which sell petrol in small glass bottles. Other stalls may sell various vegetables, fruits, and snacks, since these remote areas aren't blessed with modern convenience stores every two miles like we are used to here in the United States. Roasted corn and chestnuts are also considerably popular here, and both these items can typically be found at any food stall along the streets, even if located deep within the countryside.

This time, on the way to the salt fields, our driver was wonderful. He remained quiet as we

A Cambodian vegetable market offers a wide array of fresh foods

passed through the brightly lit city out into the cover of darkness which still gripped the remote, rural areas.

It was still pitch dark when we arrived at the salt farm, and the only lights which we saw twinkling were in the distance. The soft lights illuminated the small open-air shed where the salt workers had converged, albeit briefly, to enjoy their morning tea. Our driver was required to translate for us, since the salt workers couldn't speak a word of English. We were not on an official tour of the salt farm, and the only reason that we had been granted access to the property was because of connections I had made with a local tour guide the night before. Allow me to explain.

The previous night, determined to tour a salt farm before I leave the country, I had marched into the office of a tour agency and expressed my desire for a salt farm tour. To my dismay, the lady behind the desk informed me that this was simply not possible. There were no tours like this available.

Laden with food, a vendor walks the streets in Ho Chi Minh City

But I wasn't about to permit this woman to dash my dreams in such a casual, lighthearted manner. Especially not so flippantly as she had initially presented herself. I slowly sat down in the chair in front of her, wondering aloud if this unpleasant situation could possibly be rectified. Expecting, and rightfully so, that this situation could be resolved with money, I explained kindly that I would be willing to pay extra if she would have any connections to a salt farm that would allow an American tourist to visit for a few hours.

Smiling, she told me to wait while she called someone. After a few moments of chit-chat, she hung up and smiled very satisfactorily. "I called my husband. He knows where salt farm is. He will take you in morning. Price is three million Dong."

After running those numbers in my head for a bit, I agreed. Three million Dong it is. She signaled for me to wait once more, and then upon the conclusion of the second phone conversation, she indicated that the price would be four million. When I asked why the price jumped a million within the last two minutes, she responded that because it's an early morning trip, the driver needs an extra million. I agreed to this as well, but firmly warned her that this is as high as I would go, regarding the price.

Jeffrey and a friendly Cambodian rice farmer pose for a photograph

The streets are clogged with scholars as the schools dismiss classes for the day

Temples and monuments grace majority of the area near Battambang

A young boy walks atop the path which winds through the temples

Two young boys, cloaked in traditional orange robes, stand atop the temple steps

Monks climb hundreds of steps to worship atop this Cambodian mountain

Monuments such as these were built long before the electronic age

Prayer messages are written on this plant located near the temple

The sky is apparently the limit for loads transported by Cambodian motorbikes

The highways proved to be very interesting in Cambodia

The contents of an overloaded minivan nearly spills onto the roadway

Staying cool is essential in the tropical heat

A boy enjoys a bowl of food while hitching a ride home with his classmates

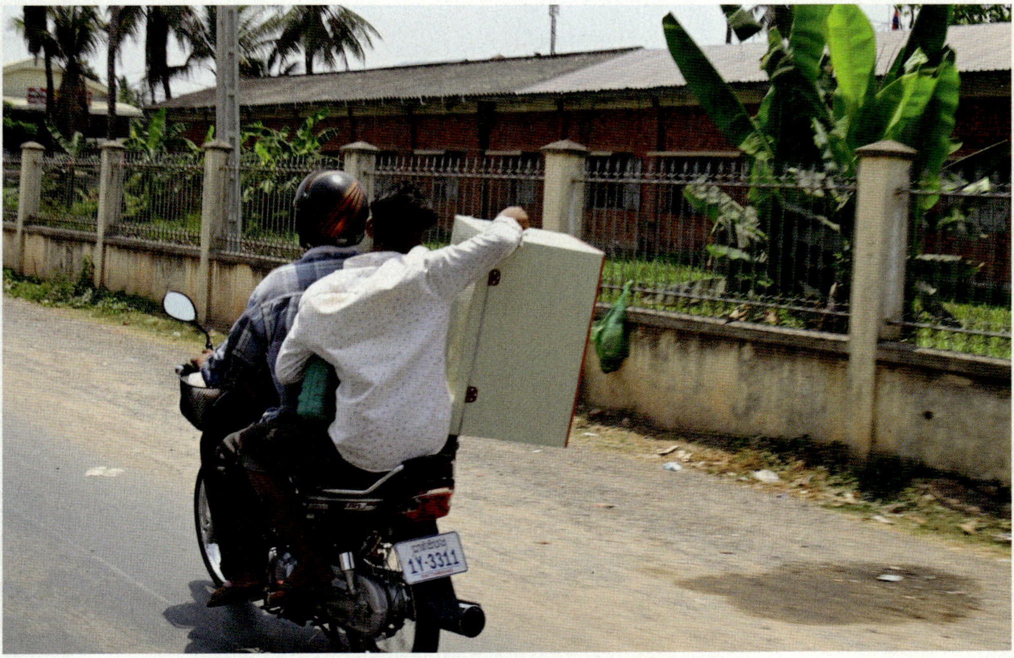

Practically anything can be hauled with the help of a friend

Navigating the streets can be a bit of a chore, but travel is made easier with one of these

Mattresses and a host of other items are stacked high on the back of a motorbike trailer

Driving with one hand while clutching the box with the other, a man carefully maneuvers the narrow side street

Children cross a bridge after classes are dismissed

Boys operate motorbikes at a young age throughout many regions of Asia

A young lady inspects her nails as she occupies a motorbike in transit

A woman lifts her feet as she clings tightly to the back of a motorbike as it hurtles through the busy streets

A woman and her son travel along a Cambodian city street

A rider is provided with a bird's eye view of the roadway atop a fast moving truck

A passenger checks his smartphone while enjoying a ride through the city

A motorbike with several young girls attemps to cross a two lane dirt highway

A man transports a hefty load of items along a Cambodian highway

A load of rubbish outside a Cambodian clinic

A beverage vendor stocks up on drinks while visiting a distribution facility

A man conducts repairs along the track which the bamboo train follows

A bamboo train outfitted with a small gasoline engine

The entrance of the Bamboo Train Ride

Students wait impatiently as a crossing guard assists them with navigating the busy streets

Scholars rejoice as they run along the dusty roads on their way home from class

A student poses for a photograph outside her school

A scholar assists a friend while zipping a backpack

A cheerful breakfast platter that the author initially balked at consuming, but then enjoyed

A vendor prepares food items she wishes to sell

A Vietnamese man repairs a chipped portion of a sidewalk

Cattle feast during the wet season and scrounge during the dry season

Malnourished cattle graze in a field near Battambang Cambodia

A young man sits on the back of a pickup truck while securing the contents of the day's work

A temple is seen in the background as cattle graze in a field

CHAPTER 13
FLOATING VEGETABLE MARKETS AND DUBAI DREAMS

To the right of the photograph, a few residents search for snails and other unique species

So, now here we were, a few hours later in the wee hours of the morning, huddled in the pre-dawn darkness, nursing a cup of hot lemongrass tea. The tea was quite potent, and nearly turned my stomach inside out. (If you ever have the chance to try lemongrass tea, politely pass on it.)

The salt shack where Jeffrey and the author tried to enjoy a cup of lemongrass tea before sunrise

My reaction to the first sip must have been humorous, because several of the farmers who were sitting beside me on the wooden bench laughed and pointed, nodding approvingly. I think they were impressed that I had been brave enough to try it; they seemed well pleased to have two uneasy American boys in their presence.

Gliding past a few baskets of salt, a worker toils in the early morning light

Dawn breaks as the backs of hardworking ladies also nearly break while carrying heavy baskets of salt

After all the tea had been consumed from the rusted tea kettle, which had been heated over a small wood fire in an open-air shanty located in the middle of a field, we walked briskly toward the area where mounds of salt littered the reflective fields. The first steaks of light were flirting heavily with the morning skies, and if the colors

Salt workers demonstrate how to properly empty the contents of their baskets

were an accurate indication of things to come, we would be witnessing a gorgeous sunrise within the hour.

Jeffrey and I observed the manual operations of the salt workers as they lifted their bamboo baskets of salt and carried it for a few steps and then emptied them onto the existing mounds of salt, which I expected might have been there for a few days. None of the salt workers could communicate with us, so we relied heavily on the translating skills of our bilingual taxi driver.

After demonstrating the proper procedures of collecting and depositing salt, the salt workers thought it would be a great idea to have us try it, too. Of course, Jeffrey and I were eager to put in a few minutes of manual labor during our visit to the Vietnamese salt fields. But perhaps we shouldn't have been so eager, since we did not

Jeffrey assists with the arduous task of harvesting salt

possess such adept skill sets as our smiling, hard-working counterparts.

Walking slowly while balancing two baskets of salt over your shoulders, and simultaneously attempting to avoid prematurely depositing the contents of the baskets, is about as difficult as it may sound. The baskets were heavy and wobbly, and we could hardly walk upright due to the heavy burden on our shoulders. The end result was less than flattering—the baskets of salt toppled over before we had hoped. This apparently tickled the salt workers, because they chuckled quite loudly for a while. For the duration of the wobbly walk, it had felt as if I was trying to keep two over-sized saltshakers from tipping over.

On the way home from the salt farms, our driver wanted to take us to a waterfront. I am glad we agreed to the additional detour, because we saw some of the most picturesque scenes in all of Vietnam.

The following day we spent most of our time walking through the city, exploring the many colorful farmer's markets. If you never have been to Vietnam, it might be surprising to learn what all is sold at a typical street market. Of course, the fare that is offered at the markets could also vary greatly and be location specific. At any cost, beware. Chicken feet and pig eyes were on full display here. As well as large slabs of meat, which weren't refrigerated. The summer sun heated the market, and flies converged hungrily on the fresh slabs of meat.

Snail stalls are a quite common sight here as well. (I am afraid you read that correctly). Snails are considered desirable cuisine here and you should have no trouble finding a food stall which will be all too eager to satisfy any cravings for snail which you might harbor.

When we inquired at our hotel's front desk what must-see sights that we should visit before we leave the

Protruding rocks dominated the rocky beaches outside Na Trang

country, we were quite adamantly advised to visit a floating vegetable market in Cai Rang.

Now, there are several floating vegetable markets in Vietnam, with the one in Cai Rang among the largest of such markets. So, after many hours of planning, it was settled. We would get up early again—this time at 4 AM—so we could observe the early morning activities of the floating market.

"You must go early in the morning, very early. The market is only open from 4 AM to 11 AM. It gets too hot after 11 AM, this is why it closes early," the concierge

A busy open-air meat and vegetable market in Cai Rang

had explained.

Well, we were more than four hours away from the market, so that meant if we wanted to catch the activities of the market at its mid-way point, we would need to leave in a taxi car before breakfast.

We arrived at the market, tired and

Poultry carcasses are strewn across a table at a meat market in Cai Rang

Flies collect on the chicken feet at an outdoor Vietnamese market

hungry, shortly after 9AM. The sun was already high and angry, and the poor farmers who were out on the water selling their vegetables, looked like they could use a break. We promptly searched for a boat that would be willing to take us out on the water, since we wanted to

experience this unique livelihood.

I am unsure of the best way to explain this situation, but I will try. Imagine, for those of you who live in Lancaster County, Weaverland Produce Auction or Leola Produce Auction conducting business on the

Interested buyers inspect the live fish before selecting their purchase

Meat is displayed in the hot open-air market

The author refrained from purchasing any of these

water instead of on land. For those of you living in areas other than Lancaster County, just imagine your local produce auction, operating in the same manner as previously described. That will give you a good idea of what we experienced.

The exact moment which we

Quite a few markets throughout Vietnam specialized in displaying meat openly. Flies unfortunately gathered around the meat

The waters are busy around Na Trang

Two men transport their circular boat across the sandy beach

found a boat headed out to the floating market, we paid the operator and quickly claimed a seat. Without delay, we were cruising toward the market in our little boat, which featured a sputtering engine. I normally might have nervously paid the weak, sputtering engine more attention, but not today. I was too enamored with the complex transactions of the floating vegetable market.

Boats loaded high with pumpkins, onions, pineapples, watermelons, squash, cucumbers, lettuce, and tomatoes sped around in the murky waters. I am probably forgetting a host of vegetables that were also sold here, other than the ones I previously mentioned, but I simply mentioned the ones that I remembered seeing.

Very shortly after we had entered the outskirts of the floating market, various boats circled ours like hawks, their owners determined to sell us some vegetables or fruit. We didn't really want to buy a large quantity of fresh produce, so we kindly declined. We did, however, reciprocate a friendly couple's offer of preparing us breakfast from their houseboat. After tethering their boat

Hearty breakfast soup which was sold for pennies (US) at the Vietnamese market

A man prepares breakfast for farmers and tourists alike from his small boat

to ours, the man fixed us a nice bowl of hot soup for breakfast, which we were so grateful for since we hadn't eaten all morning.

The soup looked nothing like the soup my mother makes, but it was still quite edible. It isn't every day that I am presented the opportunity of ordering hot soup and exceptionally stout coffee from an authentic Vietnamese vegetable farmer. I am not sure how often the paper cup had been used though, because the inside of the cup contained distinct stains and the bottom of the cup fell out before I even had the chance to enjoy more than two sips of the beverage. That was a bit disturbing as well as disappointing.

This produce market was a lot like the local markets which I frequently attend around home, with one great distinction. This produce market took place out on the water, and not on land. Instead of horse-drawn wagons and steel-wheeled tractors drumming the asphalt on their way to the local markets here in Lancaster County, old wooden boats with seemingly older engines attached to them, raced through the waters, setting off muddy waves and cloudy ripples in their wake.

Here, in similar fashion as the local markets at home, each vegetable farmer wore a hat. Not a straw hat which is such a common sight in the heart of Lancaster County, but a rice hat. Most of you have seen these hats, they are iconic to Vietnam; it is hardly easy to think of Vietnam without envisioning these wonderfully wide brimmed hats. When I glanced out upon the waters of the floating market, I had to squint due to the streaks of sunlight which reflected off the waters. But when I shielded my eyes with my hand as I held it to my forehead, I saw a most memorable scene which I won't soon forget. Dozens of rice hats appeared to be bobbing on the water as the farmers made their way across the waters in their produce-laden boats.

I had never in my life expected that I would ever see a sight like the one which I had just beheld. It was like being transported back in time, to a little-known century or millennium, where everyone lived distinctly different than what I had ever known.

A local informed us that some of the farmers live on their boats, and very rarely, if ever, do they leave the waters. To my understanding, some larger boats would simply remain docked out on the water, and every morning, farmers with smaller boats would tether their boats to the larger ones and off-load whatever fruits and vegetables the larger buyers would want.

The farmers who chose to live out on the waters in the boats, are reportedly met with many challenges. One particular challenge which stuck in my head was the following example of how the aggressive nature and intense behavior of tourists can create an imbalance in the otherwise peaceful ambiance of daily life here on the quiet waters of Vietnam. A challenge which the boat farmers face should be a simple one, but it isn't. Many times, when they wash their clothes in the river and hang them on the boat's line to dry, tourists will hawk the area and swoop in, trying to purchase the boat owner's clothing. I guess everything is for sale for the right price, right?

Mostly retail transactions take place here at the floating market, but a few decades ago, during the market's hay-day, wholesale transactions also frequently occurred.

Today, the market is a big draw for international tourists, perhaps in much the same way as any small roadside stand seems to be a magnet for tourists while they drive along the idyllic country roads of Lancaster County and the surrounding farming areas.

We slept sporadically on the long drive home, but I did catch a glimpse of the roadside action a few times throughout our four-hour taxi ride. Several times, we passed through farming communities which were graced by small rivers and canals. It became a rather common sight in Vietnam to witness small to medium sized boats gliding up to the docks of feed mills. Here, the feed mills were strategically placed along the riverbanks, allowing ease of access for the farmers who wished to fill their boats with feed for their livestock. The bulk feed was placed

The skyline of Na Trang, Vietnam is picturesque and serene

into the boats, and piled as high as possible, sometimes spilling over the sides of the boats.

The air-conditioned room in our hotel was waiting patiently for our return, and I was impatiently anticipating becoming reacquainted with the luxurious climate-controlled room. I flopped my exhausted body on the bed as soon as we entered the room and reflected on the day's wonderful scenes. Even with my head full of special memories from the events of the passing day, I still found myself with a mind filled with Dubai dreams.

I couldn't rest and reflect for too long, because I needed to schedule a ten-hour flight to a completely different area of the world. The Arabian Desert and the glittering new skyscrapers of Dubai seemed to grow increasingly eager to welcome Jeffrey and I to the final country which was on our itinerary on this global tour.

A complimentary item distributed to each passenger on the plane. Can you guess the contents within the package.

A little boy inspects the moss which beautifully covers the dock

A motorbike operator transports two dogs in a crate along a highway

A puppy tags along as its owner shops at a local market

A salt worker prepares to transport heavy baskets of salt which she gathered

Reflections in the waters created beautiful visuals as the workers carried their baskets

Bowls of colorful fruits are neatly displayed at the market

Breakfast is served differently in Vietnam. Here; duck eggs, dragonfruit, noodles, and pineapple

Colorful streets were common throughout Na Trang

Fancy desserts are prevelant and readily available at all the city cafes

Ladies, donning traditional headwear for farmers, anxiously await interested buyers of their vegetables

Notice the cardboard sign. 10,000 Dong seems like a lot for vegetables, but it really isn't

Live crabs are also tied together at the market

Live frogs are tied together by their legs at the market

Many street markets and restaurants provide their clientele with the option of purchasing live fish

Motoring past a classy hotel, a farmer travels through the city streets on his way to the market

Pizza, even though it is covered with corn in Vietnam, is quite delicious

Salt is collected on a pile where it will set until it is ready to be sold

The first streaks of morning light were thought-provokingly beautiful

Vibrant vegetables are on display at a vegetable market in Cai Rang

The only legible words and sense of familiarity is the Coca Cola sign in the background of the photograph

CHAPTER 14
CAMEL RACES, UNDERWATER HOTELS, AND INDOOR SKI SLOPES

A hotel built on a man-made island in Dubai

In case you haven't yet guessed by the title, we are no longer in the impoverished Asia territories anymore. The poor people with their floating villages and emaciated livestock is but a distant memory here. The excessive, over-indulgent lifestyles of the Dubai debonair serve as a

Glittering skyscrapers comprise Dubai's impresive skyline

stark reminder of the economic dichotomy across the globe. It is difficult to avoid getting swept up in the decadence and pomp which envelops the glittering city of Dubai.

Delectable desserts can easily break the bank in Dubai due to exorbitant and unusually agressive pricing

It was all beginning to make sense to me now. I understood why the lady at the check-in counter at Vietnam Airlines had asked us if we have adequate funds with us. Initially, I had resented her question. I had even begun to question her motives. Why was she asking me how much cash we were carrying? Why did she insist on knowing what the limits were on my credit cards? And why did she do some math when I told her that we are staying for four days in Dubai?

All these questions had needed to be answered before

Burj Khalifa, the tallest building in the world (2019)

The Grand Mosque, Abu Dhabi

she handed over our boarding passes. If I hadn't understood then, I did now. Here in Dubai, everything is priced quadruple the amount that you would expect. For example, a slim slice of cake at a diner cost $9.00, and the most I ever paid for a cup of boring black coffee broke the bank at $8.63 USD.

But we weren't about to let these excessively high prices for necessities get in the way of our otherwise enjoyable trip. We would simply curb our spending a bit and clutch our pocketbooks even closer. Up until now, we had been spoiled by the impossibly inexpensive foods and beverages throughout Asia.

Let's begin our interesting tour of Dubai at the feet of the lofty Burj Khalifa. If you are unfamiliar with this building, you might wish to keep reading. There are some unbelievable architectural achievements which crown the skies above the once-humble, sandy deserts of Dubai.

As one might expect, the world's tallest building did not disappoint. Early one hazy summer morning, in attempts to beat the throngs of tourists who descend upon the building like vultures, we scheduled a journey to the top of the Burj Khalifa. It was considerably intimidating to be transported at lighting speed in an elevator to the 148th floor. The elevators moved at a rate of nine meters per second, (yes, lightning is faster) so very little time elapsed until we had reached our lofty destination.

While we walked around on the terror-inducing, sky-high lookout deck which wrapped elegantly around the structure, we were treated to such comforts as exquisite cookies and fine teas. These treats were included in the price for a semi-private tour of the property.

A few statistics which we learned regarding the magnificent building while we were on said tour, is as follows. It takes approximately nine hours to walk up the 2,909 steps of the building. This caused me to have a sudden, greater level of respect for elevators which I hadn't previously exhibited. (Yes, someone actually climbed the entire 2,909 steps shortly after the building opened to the public. And no, they don't allow commoners to climb the steps anymore).

The total cost of the building project soared nearly as high as the building itself. More than 1.5-billion dollars was spent on the completion of this aesthetic, Arabic architectural ambition. On any given day, ten thousand people live and work in this impressive building. Everything about the structure seems to gleam with impossibility, especially the windows. A total of more than 24,000 windows comprise the elegant masterpiece which has been the pride and joy for this growing city located at the edge of the Arabian Desert. Our tour guide explained that the windows do get washed occasionally, and it takes two people three months to clean all the windows.

The building project itself progressed rather quickly, or in a much more expedient manner than what I would have initially thought. Here in Dubai, the construction of new skyscrapers takes precedent over anything else, and crews of construction workers ensure that the building projects continue around the clock. "It is different here in Dubai than most other countries," our guide explained. "Here, the construction continues 24-7. We never stop."

Perhaps that is a relative factor in the expeditious manner of which the concrete, steel, and glass emerged from the desert sands in less than six years. Twelve-thousand people, from 196 nationalities, lent their expertise in the construction of this building. You would think that after attaining such a lofty goal, a nation would be inclined to rest on their laurels. But not Dubai. They are currently working at constructing another skyscraper, this one will be double the height of the already tallest building in the world.

"We will build another one, even higher than this one," our guide declared, authoritatively. "The new building will be a mile high. Tethers will be attached, ensuring that the building will

Waters shimmer serenely in a pool at the Grand Mosque

The opulent entrance to the expansive Grand Mosque

be a success. We plan to open this new super-structure sometime in 2020. You must come back to see it. It will surely be unlike anything you have ever seen. It will make Burj Khalifa appear tiny."

A mile high? I couldn't believe it. But here they were, busily working on the foundation. Jeffrey and I saw it with our own eyes. I guess we need to start believing it.

Emaar, the Dubai-based construction company which completed the Burj Khalifa project and is working on their new mile-high project, currently has multiple building projects in the wings. According to our guide, Emaar presently has open projects which total $26 billion USD.

These ambitious projects are built on the backs of poor migrants, which primarily hail from significantly impoverished countries such as Bangladesh, Pakistan, and regions of India. More than ten million of these migrant workers raise the city's temporary population as well as its breathtaking skyline. On average, there are not nearly as many permanent residents occupying Dubai—only about four million.

But even with four million residents and several million migrants, a city needs to have abundant sources of fresh water, right? Well, since Dubai is a city located in a desert region, every gallon of water that is consumed here needs to be filtered, we were told. We were fortunate to catch a glimpse of this massive filtration facility, located far outside the city. I personally have seen a lot of things in my lifetime which caused me to shake my head in wonder and amazement at the audacity of humans, and I must say, the larger-than-life water filtration facility was one of those moments. It was quite vast. The water is collected from the Arabian Gulf, according to Rebecca, our well-spoken tour guide.

At the edge of Dubai City sets an expansive strip of land which the locals refer to as Dubai Land. Here, in Dubai Land, approximately four miles outside the city, the hazy skies are littered with tower cranes, nearly blocking out the sun itself. There are currently forty high-rise complexes and skyscrapers being constructed at present.

"Five years ago, this was all sand," Rebecca explained. "But in another five years from now, this Land will look like Dubai City. I know this to be true," she nodded emphatically, "because when I first moved here from Switzerland several years ago, Dubai City didn't look anything like it does today."

But what is fueling this expeditious growth? Well, I was told that initially it had been the trickle of oil money which originated from Dubai's sister city, Abu Dhabi. The trickle of black gold which found its way here several decades ago, has slowed significantly, since Dubai has become more independent and self-reliant. Currently, tourism accounts for majority of Dubai's income. Vacationers and wealthy folks from every corner of the world converge unto the shimmering city, in hopes to attain a unique experience.

And they won't be disappointed, because unique experiences are in abundance here. If your pockets are deep enough, you can order a filet mignon covered in 24-karat gold. Jeffery and I walked past the steakhouse which offers such an indulgence to the wealthy, which is, in a twist of irony, owned by a billionaire Dubai sheik.

I don't think that I need to convince you that all this extravagance was a bit mind-boggling for us. And maybe it is for you, too. If so, you might want to quit reading right now, because I am only really getting started in explaining the decadence that envelops Dubai.

Sand dunes in the Arabian Desert. God knows the exact number of the grains of sand in every desert on earth

Only a few animals were seen in the Arabian Desert outside Dubai

Trees provide little relief from the scorching desert heat, vegetation is equally scarce

CHAPTER 15
BEDOUIN HOSPITALITY, LIGHTNING FAST FALCONS, AND HEARTFELT GOODBYES

A camel trainer demonstrates his affection for his beloved camels

The country plays host to the world's largest mall, which just happens to also have been the most visited building on the planet in 2011. The mall is palatial, and we got lost four times within a matter of hours. It was discouraging.

Dubai Mall, the largest mall in the world (2019)

The indoor ski resort in the middle of the desert city of Dubai

Participants engage in snow fun inside the indoor ski slope in Dubai

The mall is unlike any mall in America, however, specifically regarding the customers. People of Islamic faith flood the mall, their white robes flowing gently behind them as they parade through the shops in their sandals, clutching luxury designer bags in their hands.

Women in hijabs are a common occurrence. The country is considered significantly more liberated and relaxed regarding social expectations and local laws, when compared to its highly traditional neighbor, Saudi Arabia. Still, large numbers of traditional Saudis are eager to soak in the inexplicable indulgences of their liberated neighboring country.

A worship building designed by the prince is fit for a king

Just a few more words on the mall, though. Inside one of the many malls which plague the city, is an indoor ski slope. Yep, right at the edge of the Arabian Desert you can ski indoors

Appearing new and unspoiled, the Grand Mosque impresses millions of tourists each year

on actual snow. The slope features five runs, with the longest of the five measuring four-hundred meters with a drop of sixty meters. Heavy winter jackets, gloves, and ski pants are required to enter the enclosed ski slope. Oh, and not surprisingly, you will also need to pay extravagantly to enter. After the fun is over and you are ready to head back to your hotel, you can choose from a bank of nearly three-hundred taxi cars which are lined up outside the property, winding their way around the basement level of the large building.

Opulent and palatial, the Grand Mosque cost more than $500 million to build

But there is also another notable mention here in Dubai. The Burj Al Arab Jumeriah. If

The domes of the mosque can be seen far outside the city

you are wondering why most of their exquisite buildings are named Burj, allow me to explain. Burj, in Arabic, means building. For example, the Burj Khalifa, simply translates to building Khalifa, which is named in honor of Sheik Khalifa. Now, back to the Burj Al Arab, but first, grab your snorkel, because we might need it. Because it's a luxury hotel which features a few rooms that are underwater.

The opulent hotel is only for the wealthiest of the wealthy, or so it seems. The underwater rooms feature

The expansive, elegant mosque located in Abu Dhabi, the richest city in the world (2019)

floor to ceiling windows, or so I am told. I didn't sleep here. A quick price check revealed that it wouldn't be practical to sleep in such luxury, since the only room which was available that night

Expensive diamonds and crystals hang from the ceiling inside the Grand Mosque

was priced rather exorbitantly. I shielded my eyes when I first saw the price. It hurt my eyes. $4,443.00 USD for one night. Arranging such accommodations was unthinkable, especially since we had seen the stick and plastic huts which the Lao and Cambodian folks had called home. Also, lest we forget the words of Jesus: *The foxes have holes and the birds of the air have nests, but the Son of man has not where to lay his head. (Matthew 8:20 KJV).*

During our four-day stay in Dubai, we had the opportunity to visit Abu Dhabi, the richest city in the world (2019). It is here that we engaged in a tour of the Grand Mosque. The vast, visually captivating mosque spans thirty acres and reportedly carried a completed construction cost of well-over $500 million. Completion of the gleaming, white-marbled structure took less than

The walls are elegant inside the Grand Mosque

seven years. Rare and precious jewels and diamonds, valued at several million dollars, dangle from the cathedral-styled ceiling as tourists gaze upon them in starry-eyed wonder.

You can also find other extravagant indulgences within the city of Dubai. The largest indoor aquarium, which hosts more than thirty-thousand different species of aquatic life, is waiting for you here. The world's largest high-definition video wall is also located within the mall, which boasts a record total of 1.7 billion pixels. If laid end for end, the pixels would stretch more than 11 kilometers in length.

A Land Rover travels along a path in the Arabian Desert

Here in this city, it is difficult to imagine the amounts of money that is spent simply on entertainment purposes.

Our time was quickly reaching a conclusion, and all the better, because after being away from home for nearly six weeks, both Jeffrey and I were becoming exhausted and drained. We expressed our desire to work again, to get dirt under our nails once more. The trip had been immensely educational and eventful, but all good things eventually, or so they say, must come to an end.

But there is one more highlight which I will share

Jeffery observes a falcon show from a distance

with you before we jump on a plane headed back to the United States.

A falcon rests on the gloved hand of an American tourist

On a sultry day, yes that's pretty much all there ever is here, Jeffrey and I embarked on a guided tour of the Arabian Desert. We jumped into the back of a 1961 open-air Land Rover (jeep-styled vehicle), and after our driver released some air from the tires, headed for the sandy dunes of the nearby desert.

The desert was, at least several hundred years ago, occupied primarily by nomadic Bedouin tribes. The Bedouins subscribed to the belief that they should be self-sustainable, and would typically shun any food, medicine, or help from sources outside of their desert camps. But today, most of the ancient tribesmen have assimilated into society, abandoning their deeply held beliefs as they succumbed to the encroaching pressures of society around them. In other words, their world became smaller and smaller with the advent and continuation of advancing technology.

Our guided tour did, however, provide us with a thorough glimpse of what nomadic life consisted of so many years ago. We learned that, in ancient times, when a wandering Arabic man or women approached a Bedouin camp and received a full cup of water or coffee, it was

Camels receive therapy and surgeries (if necessary) at the hospital

a sincere sign that the travelers were not welcome. A half cup indicated that the wandering traveler was permitted to stay the night.

The guide explained further how all this began. "If you were the wandering traveler who received a full glass of hot tea or water from the Bedouins, that was a strong indication that their camp was fully occupied for the night, and that you must move on. The full glass (rather than half) was considered a courtesy, which hopefully lasted for the duration of your travels upon your departure of their camp. The half glass indicated that you were permitted to stay, there was adequate space for you to stay within their camp for the night.

So, after having heard this story, Jeffrey and I never felt more welcome in our lives, because while we visited such a camp (which is, however, no longer occupied by authentic Bedouins), we were offered a half cup of coffee and tea.

The same evening which we spent cruising through the Arabian Desert in an antiquated Land Rover, we also jumped at the opportunity to observe a live falcon show. Falcons are majestic birds and can fly up to 200 mph. Today, falcons are used a lot in the Mongolian highlands, as well as in several other countries. The birds are excellent hunters, possessing impeccable eyesight. The prized hunting birds are so valuable that they even have their own passports, just like we humans. Transporting the falcons from one country to another is tricky, and virtually impossible, if the bird does not have a passport allowing them to fly in the aircraft. (Well, they aren't allowed to actually fly inside the plane, but I think you get the point).

Another highlight for us was when we bounced along the desert roads in a taxi the following day, with good intentions of meeting camel trainers. Our ill-planned excursion was looking like it would bear very little fruit, when out of nowhere, after having driven nearly ninety minutes, we approached a group of young Muslim boys who were taking a break beside the dusty road. Their camels were resting beside them, and it looked as if both man and beast were taking a much-needed break from their travels.

I instructed our taxi driver to stop the car and inquire if there was indeed a camel training facility within the area. After conversing in Arabic with the smiling boys, the driver confirmed that there was, much to our delight, a camel training facility close by.

The driver requested that one of the boys might accompany us in our car, which I agreed upon. The boy, a Sudanese refugee, promptly extended his hand, shaking our hands vigorously, while offering Jeffery and me a huge smile. He seemed thrilled to have the opportunity to show us more about his livelihood. After driving for three kilometers, our car came to a stop at the edge of a creepy-looking compound, in the middle of the desert. To be honest, it looked much more like an abandoned cell reserved for criminals than a camel training facility, but what do I know?

Camel food is stacked high inside the little barn at the edge of the desert

Anyway, my fears were once again quite ill-founded, and I began to count the many times which I had displayed a lack of trust for people which I had met during my journey. I will say this, the number I came up with is incredibly high

Curious camels observe their human trainers from a distance

A camel shuns the camera as it rests in the desert

A portion of the camel racetrack outside Dubai city

Two boys lead their camels as they prepare them to race

and for that I am sincerely ashamed. But honestly, I don't believe that it is inherently wrong to exercise some level of discretion when placing your trust in a complete stranger while in a foreign land.

Now that I have confessed, let's get on with that camel ride. The dark-skinned Sudanese camel trainer quickly showed us the farm where he and his friends care for and train the camels. Bundles of fresh grass had been cut and shipped here from a location other than the parched desert, and a water trough occupied a corner of the building. "This is where the camels are fed," our driver translated for us. "And over here, this is where they will train them later today, but not now. They are resting now."

Apparently, it was permissible to provide a curious American with a camel ride, even if they were

The racetrack in Dubai cost several hundred million dollars

Young men smile as they ride their camels toward the racetrack

resting, because that is exactly what took place a few minutes later. I will say this, the ride was fun and different, and camels must be the most awkward creatures to have ever graced the earth.

"Camels can remember you for thirty years," the driver called out to me as I left the compound while perched precariously on the camel's uninviting back. "Don't slap him, because if you do, he will remember you for the next thirty years, and will spit at you the next time you approach him."

Well, that was certainly helpful information, even though I had no intentions of slapping the poor beast or returning to this desert.

When my short camel ride was over, I knew that the magical journey I had been on was also rapidly reaching its conclusion. With sad eyes, I bid farewell to my camel training friends. One of the boys came over to us and presented his cell phone. Unsure of what he wished to do, I looked over at our driver. "He wants to take a picture with you. He is happy that you have come to see his camels."

After the short session of self-portraits had concluded, I waved goodbye to our new-found friends. Upon completing the last bend in

A young man leads his camels to the training facility

the dusty road, I glanced back one final time. I thought my eyes were deceiving me, for there stood my friend in the middle of the trail of dust which our car had kicked up, his hand extended,

Feed troughs line the wall of the barn where the lanky camels eat each day

Green vegetation is irrigated or imported from neighboring countries

Jeffrey, Leroy, and a few of the friends they met while traveling around the world

The camel hospital in Dubai

waving goodbye. The wind was tugging at his white robe, and his feet poked through his worn sandals, but his broad, sincere smile was all that seemed to matter. Never before had someone, especially a stranger, been so happy to see me. And never before had I been so sad to bid farewell to someone whom I had just met for less than an hour. The kindness and hospitality of this poor Muslim boy, who had been training camels out in the desert for the billionaire sheik, inspired me to treat everyone I meet from this point forward, with exceptional hospitality.

On our way back to the airport, we passed by the $500 million camel racing track which had been built several years ago. Each April, camel jockeys from all over the world come here to the racetrack to race their clumsy camels, in much the same manner as the Kentucky Derby is the pinnacle of performance for racehorses.

Slowing down as we approached a tall building along the road, our driver pointed with his finger and announced, "There is the camel hospital."

Sure enough, there was a camel hospital right along the outskirts of the desert. "They bring the camels here when they are sick," the

Prayer mats occupy space outside the door of the trainers' residence

The residence where several trainers share a few crowded, unfurnished rooms

driver added before we sped off into a world of sand and sun.

The next morning came way too soon. We reluctantly waved farewell to the desert which now held much more than just sand. The desert had, after all, been the source of such precious

A young man walks past the trailer-type residence

A smoggy, hazy atmosphere dominates Dubai throughout the summer months

A yacht floats along a man-made island

Buildings are constructed 24-7 in the bustling Arabian city-state

Dubai takes on the look of a futuristic city

The entrance of the exclusive camel racing club locate outside Dubai city

Dubai's most iconic hotel

Newly erected skyscrapers dot the city skyline

memories for us, and it is there that the memories of our desert-dwelling friends will live on.

Now, what did I really learn from the people I met along the way? Well, for starters, I learned that no matter how bad I think I have it, it could always be worse. When I looked upon the decadence and opulence which seemed to possess such a stranglehold on the impossibly shiny city of Dubai, I wished to judge them for their extravagance. And I very nearly did. But then I realized that if the poor, impoverished Cambodians were to pay me a visit here in Lancaster County, and see all the riches which I have and the belongings I have accumulated throughout my life, would it look any different to them? Would my lifestyle not indeed be just as extravagant to them—in much the same manner as I compared my life to the ultra-rich residents living within the city of Dubai?

I had a head full of questions and a duffel bag brimming with soiled laundry. It was obviously high time to come home.

The palace where steaks are served with gold

Now for a few quick formalities.

In February of 2019, as a curious American tourist and eyes filled with wonder, I embarked on this adventure. Several weeks later I returned as a weary traveler with a wallet full of foreign currency, a heart filled with memories, and a head drenched in dreams.

Jeffrey, it was my good pleasure to take you along on this eventful journey. Thank you for joining me on the trip of a lifetime.

And now to my friends, family, and colleagues here in the States. Please know that I am very grateful for your enduring kindness and friendship. You may never know just how special and utterly loved I feel each time I return home from traveling to foreign countries for extended periods of time, to find you waiting on me with warm smiles and eager eyes as you anticipate my eventual return. For each time I travel, no matter the distance or duration, nothing compares to seeing the faces of loved ones upon arriving home. Thank you for inspiring me to be the best person I can be. Thank you also for never allowing me to give up on my dreams.

Finally, to the many dear friends I made abroad while on this wonderful journey of mine. I want you to know that I will never forget your gracious hospitality and your unexpected kindness. My mind still travels back to you, long after I have returned to my home country. Thank you for making a difference in my life.

Without God, none of the people or things which I saw, nor the experiences I had, would matter. May all honor and glory go to Him, whom has blessed every human being so richly and abundantly with the gift of His perfect Son, Jesus.

A hazy shot taken from behind the windows of the Burj Khalifa